INTRODUCTI

I was delighted to write this book about Nottingham Forest – one of the oldest football clubs in the world, with a roll-call of famous players including Grenville Morris, Wally Ardron, Jack Burkitt, Bobby McKinlay, Ian Bowyer, John Robertson, Kenny Burns, Viv Anderson, Nigel Clough, Stuart Pearce and many more.

Forest was founded at a meeting at the Clinton Arms in Nottingham in 1865 and was originally known as 'Forest Football Club'. Its members had previously met to play a form of hockey known as 'shinney' and the name 'Forest' refers to the Forest Racecourse where the club were initially based. The club had several homes, including the cricket pitch at Trent Bridge, before finally settling at the City Ground in 1898. They played their first game in the Football League in 1892 and, apart from two seasons between 1949 and 1951 when they were members of the Third Division (North), they have never played outside the top two divisions.

The club enjoyed a record victory in 1891, when they beat Clapton 14-0, a goalscoring record for an away game in the Football League. Yet their 12-0 victory over Leicester Fosse in 1909 was one of the most surprising results. The club was in danger of being relegated at the time and their success was so unexpected that an inquiry was held to look into it. It was discovered that Forest's success had little to do with the skill of their players and more with the fact that the previous day, a number of Fosse players had celebrated a little too vigorously at the wedding celebrations of one of their team-mates! The 12-0 scoreline remains a record win in top-flight football.

Though the club had won the FA Cup in 1898 and 1959 and the Second Division championship in 1907 and 1922, their fortunes changed in 1975 when a certain Brian Clough was appointed manager. Cloughie subsequently led Forest to the League Championship in 1978 after a run of 42 matches without defeat and to two European Cups in successive years, 1979 and 1980. Under this popular manager's direction, Forest also won the Football League Cup in 1978, 1979, 1989 and 1990.

Th above is just a foretaste of the facts, memorable moments and unusual items to be found in this A to Z of a great football team.

Within these pages, I hope that there's everything the Nottingham Forest supporter ever wanted to know about his or her club from its earliest days to the present day. There's information on notable players and managers, glorious and inglorious times and many outstanding games. I hope you find all your favourites but if you wish to add your personal preferences – or even to query anything you find in this book – please write to me, care of my publisher Sigma Press.

Dean Hayes.

A

ABANDONED MATCHES

An abandoned match may be defined as one that is called off by the referee whilst it is in progress, because conditions do not permit it to be completed.

Generally speaking, far fewer matches are abandoned in modern times because if there is some doubt about the ability to play the full game, the match is more likely to be postponed.

Over the years, Forest have had League and Cup games abandoned because of fog, ice, snow and waterlogged pitches. Sadly, however, the most talked about abandoned Forest game was the FA Cup semi-final against Liverpool at Hillsborough on 15 April 1989. The game was abandoned after only a few minutes following an appalling crush of spectators at the Leppings Lane End of the ground. Ninety-five spectators were killed and over two hundred injured in one of the country's worst sporting tragedies.

ACCRINGTON

A different club from the Accrington Stanley team which joined the League in 1921, Accrington were founder members of the Football League in 1888 and resigned in 1893 after being relegated to the Second Division. They are the only founder members of the League no longer in membership.

The two clubs met in Accrington's last season in the League with Forest winning the first encounter at home on 7 January 1893, 3-0 with Alex Higgins scoring two of the goals. The Scotsman also scored Forest's goal in the return match when the two clubs drew 1-1.

ADDISON, COLIN

Joining York City in May 1957, the Taunton-born forward scored 31 goals in 97 League and Cup games before signing for Forest in January 1961 for £12,000.

A natural inside-forward, he made his Forest debut in a 2-1 win over Cardiff City before scoring both goals the following week in a 2-1 win at West Bromwich Albion.

Colin Addison

A consistent goalscorer, he was Forest's leading marksman in 1962-63, 1964-65 and 1965-66 and hit hat-tricks against Birmingham City (4-0 Home, 4 April 1964) and Sunderland (5-2 Home 24 October 1964).

He lost his place to John Barnwell at the start of the 1966-67 season and after scoring 69 goals in 176 League and Cup games, was allowed to join Arsenal. After 15 months at Highbury he joined Sheffield United before playing non-League football with Hereford United. As manager, he led the Edgar Street club to their giantkilling FA Cup run of 1971-72 before they won entry to the Football League the following season.

He later managed Durban City, Notts County, Newport County (twice), Derby County, West Bromwich Albion (twice), Atletico Madrid and Celta Viga before rejoining Hereford United for the 1990-91 season.

AGGREGATE SCORE

Nottingham Forest's highest aggregate score in any competition came in the second round of the Football League Cup in 1988-89 against Chester City when they notched up ten goals over two legs. Forest won the first leg at the City Ground 6-0 and then 4-0 at Chester's then Sealand Road ground with Tommy Gaynor grabbing a hat-trick.

ALDERSHOT

In March 1992, the liquidator who had been called in to supervise the winding up of the 'Shots' confirmed to the Football League that no offers had been received for the Fourth Division club.

The two clubs first met on 24 September 1949 in the Third Division (South) with Forest winning 3-0 before a Tommy Capel goal gave them a 1-1 draw at the Recreation Ground in the return. When Forest won the Third Division (South) championship in 1950-51 they beat

Aldershot 7-0 with Wally Ardron scoring a hat-trick, though they lost 1-0 in the away fixture.

ALLSOP, DENNIS

Goalkeeper Dennis Allsop joined Forest from Derby Junction in 1892, making his League debut in the 3-1 win at home to Wolverhampton Wanderers on Christmas Eve.

Replacing the erratic William Brown, Allsop was a highly efficient 'keeper who dominated the penalty area. Unfortunate never to have been capped by England, he was Forest's regular goalkeeper for over seven years, making 233 League and Cup appearances.

He gained a FA Cup winners' medal in 1898 when Forest beat Derby County 3-1 at the Crystal Palace. He was in outstanding form that day, saving everything that was thrown at him, including an absolute screamer from Derby's Cox.

He played his last game for the club at West Bromwich Albion on 16 April 1900 when the Reds went down 8-0, a disappointing end to what had been a glittering career.

ANDERSON, BILL

Lincoln City's most successful manager had a certain attraction for Nottingham Forest! In November 1931, he went to Forest on two months trial from County Durham. Later while playing for Barnsley, he suffered a double leg-fracture playing against Forest and in November 1966 he left Lincoln City to become assistant-manager at the City Ground.

ANDERSON, VIV

The first coloured footballer to play League football for the Reds, he made his League debut for the club on 21 September 1974 in a 3-2 win over Sheffield Wednesday at Hillsborough.

It wasn't until 1976-77 that Anderson became the club's regular right-back and scored the first of his 22 goals for the club in the 6-1 win over Sheffield United. Nicknamed 'Spider' because of his long legs, he made his England debut against Czechoslovakia in November 1978 and so became the first coloured player to gain a full England

Viv Anderson, the first coloured player to win an England cap.

cap. He remained Forest's regular right-back until the end of the 1983-84 season when he was transferred to Arsenal for £250,000.

A most popular player at the City Ground, he had made 430 League and Cup appearances in his ten years with the club, winning a League Championship medal, two League Cup winners' medals and was a member of two European Cup winning sides.

After appearing in 150 League and Cup games for the Gunners, he moved to Manchester United in 1987, again for £250,000 - the fee being fixed by an independent tribunal. Plagued by injuries during his time at Old Trafford, he appeared in 69 games before being given a free transfer and joining Sheffield Wednesday.

He is now assistant-manager to Bryan Robson at Middlesborough.

ANGLO-SCOTTISH CUP

The Anglo-Scottish Cup was inaugurated in 1975-76 following the withdrawal of Texaco from the competition of that name. Entering the competition the following season, Forest drew 0-0 with Notts

Team group 1976-77: the season that Forest won promotion to the First Division.

County, beat West Bromwich Albion 3-2 and Bristol City 4-2 to finish top of Group 'B' and qualify for the knockout stages.

Drawn against Kilmarnock, Forest won 4-3 on aggregate with Terry Curran scoring both goals in a 2-2 draw at Rugby Park, after Forest had won the home leg 2-1. In the semi-final, Forest had a comfortable 4-1 aggregate win over Ayr United. Facing Orient in the Final, a John Robertson penalty gave Forest a 1-1 draw in the first leg at Brisbane Road before goals from Barrett (2) Chapman and Bowyer gave them a convincing 4-0 win at the City Ground and the Cup!

APPEARANCES

Name	League	FA Cup	Lg Cup	Others	Total
Bob McKinlay	611(3)	53	11	7	682(3)
Ian Bowyer	425(20)	34	45(2)	37(1)	539(23)
Stuart Pearce	401	37	60	24	522
Jack Burkitt	464	37	2	0	503
John Roberston	384(14)	35(1)	46	34	499(15)
Jack Armstrong	432	28	0	0	460
Grenville Morris	423	37	0	0	460
Geoff Thomas	403	28	0	0	431
Viv Anderson	323(5)	23	39	40	425(5)
Peter Hindley	366	30	14	6	416

Consecutive Appearances: only Bob Wallace has ever made over 100 consecutive appearances for the club immediately following his debut in August 1923.

Bob Wallace made 107 appearances; debut: 25 August 1923 v Everton (Away 1-2)

Other players who have made over 100 consecutive appearances at any time during their careers with Nottingham Forest are:

Bobby McKinlay: 265 appearances from 25 April 1959 to 16 October 1965.

John Roberston: 169 appearances from 27 December 1976 to 29 November 1980

George Needham: 152 appearances from 2 September 1911 to 24 April 1915

Henry Newton: 141 appearances from 23 November 1963 to 25 March 1967

Bobby McKinlay: 135 appearances from 30 October 1965 to 14 December 1969

Billy McKinlay: 121 appearances from 25 December 1931 to 17 November 1934.

ARDRON, WALLY

Having lost much of his early football career to the Second World War, he did not enter League soccer until the age of 27 when Rotherham United signed him from Denaby United.

He made his debut for the Millmoor club in the first post-war League season of 1946-47 and impressed with his clinical finishing. A key figure in the Rotherham side that went close to promotion in the immediate post-war era, he scored 32 goals in 1948-49 to become the leading scorer in the Third Division (South).

Forest meanwhile had fallen into the Third Division (South) for the first time and manager Billy Walker was looking for a proven goalscorer to restore the club's fortunes. Ardron, who had scored 94 goals in 122 League games for the Millers, was signed in July 1949. The centre-forward scored 25 goals in his debut season but this was not enough to gain Forest promotion back to the Second Division. In 1950-51 he broke Dave 'Boy' Martin's club goalscoring record with 36 goals as Forest ran away with the title. He was the club's leading scorer in four successive seasons and scored six hat-tricks including all four goals in a 4-1 win over Hull City on Boxing Day 1952.

Many of Ardron's goals were headers, the inch perfect crosses being provided by Fred Scott. He ended his Forest career in 1955, having scored 124 League and Cup goals in 191 appearances.

ARMSTRONG, JACK

One of the country's leading experts on poultry farming, Jack Armstrong was spotted whilst playing for his home-town club, Keyworth Town. He signed for Forest in 1905 and made his Football League debut in the 4-3 win over Everton at the City Ground on 23 December 1905. Certainly the most versatile player in the club's early history, he appeared in every position for Forest except goalkeeper and fullback during his 18 years at the City Ground, although his best position was at wing-half.

An ever-present in 1907-08, 1910-11 and 1919-20, he eventually surpassed Grenville Morris' League appearance record and for the last three years of his career at the City Ground, he was made captain.

He made 460 League and Cup appearances for the Reds, but it would have been many more if it had not been for the fact that the League programme was suspended due to the First World War.

ARTIFICIAL LIGHT

On 28 October 1878, Nottingham Forest were beaten 2-1 in a match with a Birmingham representative side under artificial light, provided by a dozen electric lights spaced out around the pitch!

ASHTON, PERCY

Goalkeeper Percy Ashton joined Nottingham Forest in 1930 from Melton Excelsior as cover for Alf Dexter. He made his League debut for Forest on 13 September 1930 as the Reds beat Stoke City 3-0 in a Second Division match. However, despite that successful start, he had to wait until the 1933-34 season before he won a regular place in the side.

A consistent though unspectacular 'keeper, he was liable to make the odd mistake and in the match against Burnley on 7 May 1938 it was his mistake that gave the Yorkshire side the lead in that epic relegation battle.

Playing the last of his 185 first team games at the end of the 1938-39 season, his career was ended by the outbreak of the Second World War in September 1939.

ATTENDANCES

Attendance figures at the City Ground provide some interesting statistics:

Highest in the Football League:

Date	Opponents	Competition	Attendance
28.10.1967	Manchester United	Division One	49,946
12.10.1957	Manchester United	Division One	47,654
26.12.1977	Liverpool	Division One	47,218
25.02.1967	Leicester City	Division One	47,188
22.08.1967	Coventry City	Division One	44,951

27.08.1958	Manchester United	Division One	44,721
02.01.1978	Everton	Division One	44,030
14.01.1967	Leeds United	Division One	43,899
16.01.1965	Manchester United	Division One	43,009
27.12.1971	Arsenal	Division One	42,750

Lowest Attendances (since Second World War):

16.11.1960	Bristol City	League Cup	3,690
05.10.1960	Halifax Town	League Cup	4,422
02.05.1955	West Ham United	Division Two	5,675
29.04.1950	Port Vale	Division Three (S)	5,826
26.03.1955	Doncaster Rovers	Division Two	6,410
19.09.1972	Cardiff City	Division Two	6,414

The club's lowest ever attendance is 2,624 when West Bromwich Albion visited the City Ground on 30 March 1904.

Other games at the City Ground:

08.04.1967	Everton	FA Cup Rd 6	47,510
29.01.1958	West Bromwich Albion	FA Cup Rd 4(R)	46,477
18.02.1967	Newcastle United	FA Cup Rd 4	45,962
11.03.1967	Swindon Town	FA Cup Rd 5	45,878
28.02.1959	Bolton Wanderers	FA Cup Rd 6	45,000
01.03.1930	Sheffield Wednesday	FA Cup Rd 6	44,166
27.01.1962	Sheffield Wednesday	FA Cup Rd 4	44,044
24.01.1959	Tooting & Mitcham	FA Cup Rd 3(R)	42,236
27.01.1974	Manchester City	FA Cup Rd 4	41,472
27.02.1978	Queen's Park Rangers	FA Cup Rd 5 (R)	40,097

Nottingham Forest's average home attendances over the last ten years have been as follows:

1988-89	20,785
1989-90	20,606
1990-91	22,137
1991-92	23,721
1992-93	21,910
1993-94	23,051
1994-95	23,633
1995-96	25,916
1996-97	24,578
1997-98	20,584

AWAY

Best Away Wins

Date	Opponents	Competition	Score
23.09.1980	Bury	League Cup	7-0
02.02.1957	Port Vale	Division Two	7-1
01.04.1995	Sheffield Wednesday	Premier League	7-1
20.10.1900	West Bromwich Albion	Division One	6-1
27.01.1951	Crystal Palace	Division Three	6-1

Worst Away Defeats

10.04.1937	Blackburn Rovers	Division Two	1-9
29.09.1962	Tottenham Hotspur	Division One	2-9
16.04.1900	West Bromwich Albion	Division One	0-8
29.11.1913	Leeds City	Division Two	0-8
21.11.1959	Burnley	Division One	0-8
04.11.1922	Burnley	Division One	2-8
01.05.1926	Oldham Athletic	Division Two	3-8

Most Away Wins in a Season: 14 in 1950-51 (Div Three South)

Fewest Away Wins in a Season: 0 in 1895-96 (Division One); 0 in 1913-14 (Division Two)

Most Away Defeats in a Season: 17 in 1913-14 (Division Two)

Fewest Away Defeats in a Season: 3 in 1977-78 (Division One); 3 in 1978-79 (Division One)

Most Away Goals in a Season: 53 in 1950-51 (Div Three South)

Fewest Away Goals in a Season: 8 in 1895-96 (Division One)

BAKER, JOE

One of the most popular players ever to wear the red of Nottingham Forest, Joe Baker joined the City Ground club from Arsenal in March 1966 for a club record fee of £65,000. Though he was born in Liverpool, he had a broad Scottish accent after spending much of his early life in Motherwell. He played his early football with Coltness United and Armadale Thistle before joining Hibernian in 1956. He became a prolific goalscorer with the Easter Road club, once scoring nine goals in a game before Italian giants AC Torino secured his services in May 1961.

A year later he returned to these shores to sign for Arsenal for £70,000, at the time a record fee for the Gunners. Baker scored 100 goals in 156 League and Cup games for the Highbury outfit before joining Forest.

An England international, he made his debut on 8 March 1966 in a 1-0 win over Burnley at the City Ground. Baker became an immediate hit and was nicknamed 'The King'. He was the club's top scorer in 1967-68 with 21 goals but in July 1969 after scoring 49 goals in 135 first team games; manager Gillies sold Baker to Sunderland.

In 1970 he returned to Scotland to play for Raith Rovers before later becoming manager-coach at Albion Rovers.

BARNWELL, JOHN

An amateur with the famous Bishop Auckland team, John Barnwell attracted the attention of a number of Football League clubs before signing for Arsenal in November 1956. It was whilst doing his National Service in the RASC that he was chosen to represent the British Army. At Highbury he made 151 League and Cup appearances and won one England Under-23 cap.

He joined Forest in March 1964 for £30,000 and made his debut in a 3-2 win over Sheffield Wednesday at the City Ground that month. One of the game's first true midfield players, he settled into a deep-lying linking role and in his six seasons with Forest, scored 25 goals in 201 League and Cup appearances.

He was transferred to Sheffield United at the end of the 1969-70 season but after just nine appearances for the Blades he left Bramall Lane to coach at Hereford United and later Peterborough United. Barnwell later took charge of 'Posh', Wolverhampton Wanderers (whom he led to a 1-0 victory in the 1980 League Cup Final against Forest), AEK Athens, Notts County and Walsall.

BARRATT, PERCY

Spotted playing local football for Annesley St Alban's just after the First World War, he was signed by Forest and made his League debut at home to Stockport County in September 1919. After impressing in his first season, in which he played 21 games, he lost his place on Harry Bollings return from injury and over the next few seasons appeared in only 18 matches. Having played the bulk of these matches at right-back, he returned to prominence in 1924-25, playing at left-back and partnering Bill Thompson.

Possessing a powerful shot with either foot, he scored some spectacular goals and was the club's regular penalty-taker. Although he appeared in one match during 1929-30, an injury sustained in the 1-0 home defeat by Grimsby Town on 5 January 1929 forced his retirement from the game.

BARRETT, JIM

The son of Jim Barrett who had a long and distinguished career with West Ham United before the Second World War, young Jim also entered League football with the Upton Park club. He made his debut for the Hammers in February 1949 aged just 18 and had scored 25 goals in 87 League appearances when Forest signed him in December 1954.

Making his debut against Birmingham City, he went on to score eight goals in his 19 games that season. For his first three seasons at the City Ground, he was the club's leading goalscorer and in 1956-57 he scored 30 League and Cup goals in 37 games. During that campaign he scored in 14 out of 16 League games and hit three hat-tricks against Fulham (Home 3-1), Port Vale (Away 7-1) and Goole Town (Home 6-0).

Though he was still at Forest in 1959, he did not figure in the FA Cup side, only playing in three League games. In September 1959 he joined Birmingham City but things did not work out for him and after only ten League games he returned to West Ham but ended his career without appearing in the Hammers' League side again.

BARRINGTON, JIMMY

Born at Lower Ince, near Wigan, left-back Jimmy Barrington was playing with Wigan Borough when he wrote to the Forest asking for a trial. He was invited to the City Ground later in that year of 1929 and made his League debut at Millwall on 21 September in a 2-2 draw.

A slightly-built defender, he packed a tremendous shot, yet in 229

League and Cup games for Forest he only scored one goal and that came in a 4-2 defeat at Bury in 1933-34.

At the end of the 1935-36 season he was given a free transfer but after Forest fans had made their feelings known, he was reinstated, though he only played in one further game for the Reds. After his retirement from the first-class game, he continued to serve the club as a scout.

BARRON, JIM

Signed by Wolverhampton Wanderers in 1961, he made only eight first-team appearances during three seasons at Molineux before moving to Chelsea. Understudy to Peter Bonetti at Stamford Bridge he joined Oxford United in March 1966 and went on to play in 165 League and Cup games for the Manor Ground club. When Oxford won 1-0 at the City Ground in the fourth round League Cup tie in 1969, Barron impressed the Forest officials so much that the following summer they signed the Durham-born 'keeper for £35,000 as cover for Alan Hill.

He made his debut in the opening game of the 1970-71 season in a goalless draw at Ipswich Town and was one of five ever-presents that season, keeping 10 clean sheets. Transferred to Swindon in 1974 after 180 first-team appearances for the Reds, he later ended his career with Peterborough United.

Jim Barron shows a safe pair of hands.

BASSETT, DAVE

As a player, Dave Bassett failed to make the grade with both Watford and Chelsea and so moved into non-League football with Walton and Hersham. He played in the FA Amateur Cup Final when Walton beat Slough Town 1-0 in 1973.

In 1974 he moved to Wimbledon when they were playing in the Southern League. The 'Dons' went on to win the Premier League title in the next three seasons and in 1977 were elected to the Football League. He made 35 League appearances for the Dons before retiring to become the club coach in 1979.

He took over as manager in January 1981 and in his first season led the club to promotion to the Third Division. Despite being relegated the following season, the Dons won the Fourth Division in 1982-83 and finished runners-up in the Third Division the following season. In 1985-86 the club won promotion to the First Division and in their first season, finished third.

In May 1984 Bassett joined Crystal Palace but within a week he had changed his mind and returned to Plough Lane. Elton John persuaded him to take charge at Watford but it was an unhappy time for him and in February 1988 he joined Sheffield United.

He spent seven years at Bramall Lane before becoming manager of Crystal Palace but in February 1997 he left Selhurst Park to join Nottingham Forest as general manager, relieving caretaker player-manager Stuart Pearce of administration duties. In My 1997 he took over as team manager and in 1997-98 led Forest to the First Division championship.

A motivator of the highest order, Forest fans will be hoping that Dave Bassett can lead the club on to further glories.

BEATTIE, ANDY

A Scottish international, he has probably been involved with more clubs than any other person in the history of English football. Playing for local clubs Inverurie Rovers and Locos whilst working as a quarry-man in the town, it was from the latter that he joined Preston North End in March 1935. He appeared for the Lilywhites in the 1937 and 1938 FA Cup Finals and won seven Scottish caps between April 1937 and December 1938, plus another five in wartime internationals.

Andy Beattie

During the war he played for both Forest and Notts County as a guest. On retirement from playing, Beattie's first managerial position was with Barrow but after producing a new-found team spirit, which resulted in the club, finishing seventh in the League, he had a disagreement with the club's chairman. He resigned but was reinstated when the other directors forced the chairman to leave instead. After moving to Stockport County in a similar capacity, he was enticed to Leeds Road in April 1952 and although he was too late to stave off relegation, he guided them to promotion the following season. In 1953-54 he led the Terriers to third in the First Division.

He served twice as team manager of Scotland, once in 1954 when he took them to the World Cup finals in Switzerland and for a brief period in 1959-60.

He had resigned at Huddersfield in 1956 and had a short spell with Carlisle United before replacing Billy Walker at the City Ground in September 1960. His three years at Forest were not outstanding, with the Reds losing their first seven League games in which he was in charge. In his three seasons with the club, the Reds finished 14th, 19th and ninth before in July 1963 he resigned.

A month later he joined Plymouth Argyle as caretaker manager and saved them from relegation by the slimmest of margins. He was next caretaker manager at Molineux but after Wolves had lost 9-3 at Southampton and the illness of his wife, he resigned.

In December 1965 he joined Notts County as general manager and was in charge of team affairs when Jack Burkitt was taken ill a year later. He had coaching and scouting posts with Sheffield United, Brentford, Wolves, Walsall and Liverpool at various times. Enjoying a long, successful career in the game, he left his mark on many clubs in the Football League.

BELTON, JACK

Loughborough-born Jack Belton started his footballing career with Quorn Emmanuel FC before moving on to Loughborough Corinthians where he became a prolific goalscorer.

In 1914 he was invited to the City Ground for a trial and impressed so much that he was offered professional terms. He made his League debut for the club on 19 September 1914 in a 1-0 home defeat by Bristol City before going on to score seven goals in his 23 appearances that season. However, war was declared and at the end of his first campaign in the Forest side, League soccer was suspended.

He didn't return to the club until mid-October 1919 when the Football League had just resumed. Though he had played all his games at centre-forward, he covered at right-half for the injured Joe Mills and it was in this position that the hardworking Belton eventually found a regular place in the Forest side. He missed very few games until 1928 when after playing in 347 League and Cup games for Forest, he retired.

BEST STARTS

Nottingham Forest were unbeaten for the first 16 games of the 1978-79 season when they won seven and drew nine of their matches before losing 2-0 at Anfield. They lost only three of their 42 League matches that season, finishing as runners-up to Liverpool.

BIRTLES, GARRY

A carpet fitter by trade, Nottingham-born Garry Birtles signed for Forest from Long Eaton United in December 1976. After making his debut on 12 March 1977 in a 2-0 win over Hull City, he didn't play again until 9 September 1978 by which time Forest were in the First Division. Replacing Peter Withe, he ended that season as top scorer with 14 goals. He also scored regularly in the League and European Cups to finish the campaign with 26 goals from 53 games.

He won the first of his three England caps in May 1980 and played in the European Championships later that summer. At the beginning of the following season, he signed for Manchester United for £1.25 million but the move was not a success and after just 64 first team appearances he was back at the City Ground for a cut price fee of £250,000.

Hampered by injuries, it wasn't until 1986-87 that he **again** emerged as a goalscorer, linking well with Nigel Clough to score 15 goals in 33 games. Most Forest fans were surprised at the end of that season when he was given a free transfer and joined Notts County. He later played for Grimsby Town and starred in a back-four role for the Mariners.

Gary Birtles, seen here scoring one of his 70 league goals for the club.

BOWYER, IAN

Ellesmere Port-born Ian Bowyer started his career with Manchester City where he made his name as a goalscoring teenager. After things began to turn sour for him, he left to join Orient but two years later, Dave Mackay signed him for Forest.

He made his debut for the Reds in a 2-2 draw at Blackpool, scoring Forest's second goal but after beginning well, he suffered something of a goal drought. BY 1975-76 he had recovered his form and was the club's leading scorer with 16 goals in 46 first team appearances. The following season he missed just one game as Forest won promotion to the First Division.

A versatile player, he became the club's first-choice replacement for virtually any position after he lost his place in midfield to Archie Gemmill.

In January 1981 he left for Sunderland but a year later, after making just 15 League appearances for the then Roker Park club he returned to the City Ground. The following season he was awarded the captaincy and went on to score 97 goals in 562 League and Cup games before joining Hereford United, later becoming their manager.

BRADFORD PARK AVENUE

Park Avenue enjoyed 47 seasons in the League before failing to hold on to their place in 1969-70 after three consecutive seasons at the bottom of the League. They started their career in the Second Division in 1908-09 and in 1914 joined their Bradford neighbours City in the First Division.

The two clubs first met on 16 December 1911 when goals from Derrick and Hooper gave Forest a 2-1 win. The following season Park Avenue completed the 'double' over Forest, winning 3-1 at home and 2-1 at the City Ground. Park Avenue were relegated in 1920-21 and the following season suffered the embarrassment of dropping into the Third Division (North). They returned to the Second Division in 1928 and over the next five seasons won all their home fixtures against Forest, scoring 22 goals in the process. Forest did have one success in 1931-32 when they beat Park Avenue 6-1 with Johnny Dent grabbing a hat-trick. Another hat-trick hero for Forest in these fixtures was Eric Stubbs as the Reds won 4-1 at Park Avenue in February 1936. Tommy Johnston hit three goals on the last day of the 1946-47 season as Forest

Ian Bowyer, Nottingham Forest captain, leads out the side.

won 4-0 at the City Ground. The two clubs last met in 1948-49 when Forest were relegated to the Third Division (South) with the Reds completing the 'double' over their Yorkshire opponents who were relegated themselves in 1950-51. Founder members of the Fourth Division in 1958 they won promotion just once before their eventual demise.

BROTHERS

There have been a number of instances of brothers playing for Nottingham Forest. Among the more famous are Frank and Fred Forman who were both capped for England at the same time. Frank went on to appear in 256 first team games for the Reds and in later life was elected a life member. Fred Forman appeared in 181 first team games for Forest.

The bond between Arthur and Adrian Capes was so great that the Burton Wanderers players would only sign for Forest if the other brother did so. Injury and illness ruined Adrian's career and he only played in 33 first team games for the Reds but Arthur 'Sailor' Capes as he became known played in 191 League and Cup games, scoring 42 goals, including two in the FA Cup Final of 1898.

Jim Iremonger soon made a name for himself as a full-back and won caps for England during his 300 game career with Forest. Towards the end of his career at the City Ground, he played in goal, as did his brother Harry, who played between the sticks in 11 games between 1914 and 1915.

BROWN, ALLAN

Unfortunate with injuries, Allan Brown twice had to miss FA Cup Finals for Blackpool, though he eventually appeared in a Wembley Final for Luton Town in 1959 when Forest beat them 2-1. He had played in one of East Fife's most successful sides, appearing in two Scottish Cup Finals for the club in 1950.

He played in the 1954 World Cup for Scotland and but for injuries would have won more than 14 caps. After ending his playing career with Portsmouth, he started in management with Cheshire League side, Wigan Athletic. They won the competition once and also finished as runners-up. Also under his management, the Latics won four trophies in a season and went 52 games without defeat!

Luton Town saw his potential and appointed him manager in November 1966 when they were second from bottom of the Fourth Division. Two years later he led the Hatters to the Fourth Division championship and they were on the way to promotion again when he was sacked after applying for the vacant post at Leicester City. He moved to Torquay United in January 1969 and then Bury in June 1972. The Shakers were on the verge of the Third Division promotion race when Brown jumped at the chance of winning promotion to the First Division with Forest.

In his first season in charge, the Reds finished seventh in the Second Division and enjoyed a memorable FA Cup run. The club sank lower the following season and after 14 months in charge he was dismissed. He later managed Southport and Blackpool but the Seasiders were relegated in each of his two spells at the club.

BULLING, HARRY

Harry Bulling played football for Bridgford Juniors before signing professional forms for Heanor Town. After turning in some impressive performances at full-back, he signed for Southern League Watford where he spent four seasons up to the outbreak of the First World War.

He returned to his home-town club during the hostilities and made his League debut for Forest in the opening game of the 1919-20 season at Rotherham. However in the game at home to Grimsby on 4 February 1920, he suffered an injury from which he did not return until 1920-21.

Forming an exceptional full-back partnership with Harry Jones, he was an ever-present during Forest's Second Division championship season of 1921-22 and unlucky never to play for England.

He continued to serve Forest until 1925 when Bill Thompson arrived on the scene, playing the last of his 199 League and Cup games on 2 May in the final game of the season. On his retirement he stayed in the city, but sadly died a few months short of his 40th birthday.

BURKITT, JACK

Beginning his football career as a centre-half with Darlaston, he switched to wing-half following his move to Forest in May 1947. Breaking into the first team during the 1948-49 season after some impressive performances in the reserves, he made his League debut at Coventry City on 30 October 1948.

Along with Bill Morley and Horace Gager, he helped form the great Forest half-back line of the 1950s and was an ever-present in three seasons, 1952-53, 1955-56 and 1956-57. The Wednesbury-born player went on to break the club's League appearance record and when he played his last game for the club at Manchester City in October 1961, he had appeared in 503 League and Cup games for the Reds.

A great servant to Forest, he was the Reds' club captain for much of his career and it was he who lifted the FA Cup when they beat Luton Town 2-1 in 1959.

He retired from the playing side of the game at the end of the 1961-62 season to take up a coaching position at the City Ground. Later he became trainer at the Baseball Ground during Brian Clough's early days in management and also managed Notts County, though it has to be said, without much success.

BURNS, KENNY

Though he began his career with Glasgow Rangers, it was with Birmingham City that Kenny Burns first came to prominence. A goalscorer with more than his fair share of disciplinary problems, he had scored 45 goals in 170 League games for the St Andrew's club when Brian Clough signed him for Forest in the summer of 1977.

Playing solely as a defender, he made his debut for Forest in the 3-1 win at Everton on the opening day of the 1977-78 season. Only missing the last game of the season at Anfield, Burns was outstanding as Forest won the League Championship and League Cup. He was selected as the Football Writers' Association Player of the Year and went to Argentina with the Scotland World Cup squad. He won 12 caps during his stay at the City Ground and a total of 20 in his career.

After winning a League Championship medal, League Cup winners' medal and two European Cup medals, the popular Scotsman was transferred to Leeds United in September 1981. He had appeared in 196 League and Cup games, scoring 15 goals. After Elland Road, he played for Derby County, Notts County and Barnsley before playing non-League football with Sutton Town, Stafford Rangers and Heanor Town.

Kenny Burns, Football Writer's Association Player of the Year in 1977-78.

BURTON, NOAH

Playing his early football with Bulwell St Alban's and Ilkeston United, he signed amateur forms for Derby County in 1915 before guesting for Forest during the First World War. He scored the goal that won the club the Victory Shield in 1919 but when peacetime football resumed, he returned to the Baseball Ground.

He signed for Forest in June 1921 and made his debut in the opening game of the following season. Instrumental in the Reds winning the Second Division title in that 1921-22 season, he was one of the most popular players at the City Ground.

Though not the most prolific of goalscorers, he scored 62 goals in 362 League and Cup appearances and netted a hat-trick in Forest's 7-0 win over Fulham on 29 August 1927.

Noah Burton was also a great character off the field, having a fine singing voice and being known to be something of a comedian.

BURTON UNITED

One of the founder members of the Second Division as Burton Swifts in 1892, they merged with Burton Wanderers (after they left the League) to form Burton United. They failed to gain re-election after finishing bottom of the Second Division in 1906-07. That was the only season the two clubs met, with Forest completing the 'double', winning both matches 2-0.

C

CAMPBELL, KEVIN

A product of South London Schools, Kevin Campbell smashed all Arsenal goalscoring records in 1987-88 when finding the net 59 times for the youth team and was a prominent member of the Gunners' FA Youth Cup winning side. It was this form that earned him his League debut on the last day of that season against Everton at Goodison Park.

With Merson and Smith holding down the regular striking positions in Arsenal's 1988-89 League Championship winning season, he was loaned to Leyton Orient, whose manager Frank Clark wanted to sign him on a permanent basis. After another loan spell, this time with Leicester City, he began to establish himself in the Arsenal side, playing alongside a variety of striking partners.

In 1992-93 he was a member of the victorious double Cup winning team, scoring 14 times in 37 games and of the European Cup Winners' Cup team when he scored four times on route to the final. He had scored 60 goals in 233 League and Cup games when in for summer of 1995 he joined Frank Clark at Nottingham Forest for a fee of £2.5 million, a figure set by a tribunal.

Replacing Stan Collymore, he suffered in his first season at the City Ground with a long-standing back problem but he began 1996-97 with a hat-trick on the opening day of the season at Coventry City before receiving an injury which kept him out of the side for some time. There is no doubt that 1997-98 was his best season. Forming a deadly partnership with Pierre Van Hooijdonk, he scored 23 League goals, including a hat trick in a 4-1 win at Crewe Alexandra. He had scored 35 goals in 93 League and Cup games when he left the club in the summer of 1998 to join Trabzonspor.

CAPACITY

The total capacity of the City Ground in 1997-98 was 30,602.

CAPEL, TOMMY

After starting his League career with Manchester City just after the Second World War, he was soon transferred to Chesterfield, where he teamed up with his brother Fred. In the 1949 close season, he joined Birmingham City but after just eight appearances for the St Andrew's club, he was snapped up by Billy Walker for £14,000.

His best season for Forest came in the club's 1950-51 promotion-winning season when he scored 23 goals in 35 League appearances. He was the club's joint leading goalscorer in 1953-54 with 18 goals including a hat-trick in the 4-1 win over Fulham at the City Ground on 13 February 1954.

Surprisingly at the end of that season he was transferred to Coventry City along with his left-wing partner Colin Collindridge. After 36 games for the Sky Blues in which he scored 19 goals, he ended his League career with Halifax Town before moving into non-League football with Heanor Town.

CAPES, ARTHUR

Signed from Second Division Burton Wanderers in the close season of 1896, he went on to give Forest six years service before joining Stoke. He and his brother Adrian were both forwards with the Burton club and such was the bond between the two that Adrian would only sign if his brother came as well. Arthur was not in the same class as his brother and though this put a number of clubs off, it did not deter Forest. Unfortunately, Adrian's career was ruined through illness and injury but 'Sailor' Capes as Arthur became known enjoyed great success at the City Ground.

Making his debut in the opening game of the 1896-97 season, he went on to appear in 191 first team games for Forest, scoring 42 goals. Though he was more of a goal-maker than a goalscorer, he did score twice when Forest beat Derby County 3-1 in the 1898 FA Cup Final. In the close season of 1902 he joined Stoke, where he was capped once for England and represented the Football League. He later played for Bristol City and Swindon Town before retiring from the game.

CAPS

The most-capped player in the club's history is Stuart Pearce who won 76 caps for England.

CAPS (ENGLAND)

The first Nottingham Forest player to be capped by England was AC Goodyer against Scotland in 1879. The most capped player is Stuart Pearce.

CAPS (NORTHERN IRELAND)

The first Nottingham Forest player to be capped by Northern Ireland was John Hanna against Scotland in 1912. The most capped player is Martin O'Neill.

CAPS (REPUBLIC OF IRELAND)

The first Nottingham Forest player to be capped by the Republic of Ireland was Noel Kelly against Luxembourg in 1954. The most capped player is Roy Keane.

CAPS (SCOTLAND)

The first Nottingham Forest player to be capped by Scotland was Stewart Imlach against Hungary in 1958. The most capped player is John Robertson.

CAPS (WALES)

The first Nottingham Forest player to be capped by Wales was Grenville Morris against Scotland in 1899. The most capped players are Grenville Morris and Ronnie Rees.

CAPTAINS

Among the many players who have captained the club are John MacPherson who signed for Forest in May 1891 and was an ever-present the following season when the Reds reached the semi-final of the FA Cup. He then rejoined Hearts where he had won his one full cap against England before returning to Forest in September 1892 for the club's first Football League campaign. He was appointed club captain in 1894 and four years later led the club to success in the FA Cup when they beat Derby County in the final.

Leading scorer Grenville Morris spent the last five years of his Forest career as captain, whilst long-serving Jack Armstrong was made club captain after the war, for his final three years at the City Ground.

Jack Burkitt was Nottingham Forest's club captain for many seasons and it was he who lifted the FA Cup at Wembley in 1959 when the Reds beat Luton Town 2-1.

Club record holder for the most League appearances, Bobby McKinlay was appointed club captain in 1962 and held the position for four years until succeeded by Welsh international Terry Hennessey.

John McGovern skippered the Nottingham Forest side, which won the European Cup in successive years. He had joined the Reds from Leeds United, the fourth time he had linked up with Brian Clough.

Stuart Pearce has been highly successful in leading Forest to the Simod Cup in 1987-88, the League Cup in 1988-89 and 1989-90 and the Zenith Data Systems Cup in 1991-92.

CAREY, JOHNNY

Johnny Carey arrived at Old Trafford in 1936 after being spotted by United's chief scout, Louis Rocca. He later declared 'No greater Irish player crossed the Channel to make a name in English football.'

He made his debut at inside-forward in 1937-38 helping United to runners-up in the Second Division and then playing in 32 First Division matches the following season.

After the war, Matt Busby converted Carey to full-back and made him captain. Carey turned out against England in two international matches within three days and for different countries! He played for Northern Ireland in Belfast on 28 September 1946 and for the Republic of Ireland in Dublin on 30 September.

He led United to victory in the 1948 FA Cup Final over Blackpool and was voted Footballer of the Year in 1949. The following year he was voted Sportsman of the Year and in 1951-52 he led the Old Trafford side to the League title.

After leaving United he became manager of Blackburn Rovers. Things went well at Ewood, Carey taking the club into the First Division. This attracted the attention of Everton and after three years in charge at Goodison, he was cruelly dismissed one Christmas Eve. He took over at Leyton Orient and brought them out of the Second Division, though they went down again after one season.

He arrived at the City Ground in July 1963 and brought in such fine players as Joe Baker, John Barnwell, Terry Hennessey, Alan Hinton and Frank Wignall.

In 1966-67, Forest finished the season as runners-up in the First Division but in December 1967, Carey made his biggest mistake in paying £100,000 to bring Jim Baxter to the City Ground. A year later, Carey was dismissed with Forest having won only one of their 19 League games. He returned to Blackburn as administrative manager but as Rovers went into the Third Division for the first time in their history, he was dismissed.

CENTENARY

Nottingham Forest celebrated their centenary in 1965-66, thus becoming the third club to do so. The club arranged a celebratory match against Valencia before which a set of shirts was handed over to Forest chairman Fred Sisson by his Arsenal counterpart D.J. Hill-Wood in return of a similar gesture by Forest in 1886. Forest drew the match 1-1. The season itself was a poor one with Forest finishing in 18th place in the First Division.

CENTRAL COMBINATION

Forest's reserves spent just two seasons in the Central Combination in the mid 1930s, winning the championship in 1933-34 and scoring

131 goals. The following season, they ended the campaign as runners-up, scoring 98 goals before leaving to join the Midland League. Forest's all-time record in the Central Combination is:

P.	W.	D.	L.	F.	A.
60	41	9	10	229	74

CENTRAL LEAGUE

The Central League originated in 1911 to serve primarily the clubs in the North and Midlands reserve teams. Nottingham Forest joined the competition in 1967-68 and spent 15 seasons in the Central League until in the early 1980s, a decision was taken to have two divisions.

Despite finishing fourth in 1981-82, Forest found themselves in Division Two. However, the Reds bounced back immediately winning the Championship wit the following record:

P.	W.	D.	L.	F.	A.	Pts
30	22	3	5	66	27	47

Forest continued to be one of the stronger teams in the First Division of the Central League and won the title two years in succession with the following records:

	P.	W.	D.	L.	F.	A.	Pts
1987-88	34	25	2	7	81	37	77
1988-89	34	20	6	8	83	45	66

They then finished runners-up for the next two seasons before winning the Central League First Division title again in 1991-92:

P.	W.	D.	L.	F.	A.	Pts
34	23	7	4	81	34	76

Following the decision to restructure the Pontins League into four divisions, Forest found themselves in the Premier League and after finishing ninth in 1996-97 just avoided relegation last season, finishing five points ahead of relegated Tranmere Rovers.

CENTURIES

Goals

Nottingham Forest have scored a century of goals in a Football League season on one occasion. The club scored 110 goals in 1950-51 when they won the Third Division (South) championship.

There are six instances of individual players who have scored a hundred or more goals for Forest. Grenville Morris is the greatest goalscorer with 217 strikes in his career at the City Ground (1898-1913). Other century scorers are Nigel Clough (128), Wally Ardron (124), Johnny Dent (122), Ian Storey-Moore (118), and Enoch West (100).

Appearances

Only Bob Wallace has made over 100 consecutive appearances immediately after making his Football League debut.

CHAMPIONSHIPS

Nottingham Forest have won a divisional championship on five occasions.

1906-07 Division Two

After suffering relegation for the first time the previous season, the club returned to the top flight as Second Division champions a year later. After losing their opening game of 1907, 4-2 at Burslem Port Vale, the Reds went 17 games without defeat to the end of the season, winning 15 of them. The club's top scorer was Grenville Morris with 21 goals in 37 appearances.

P.	W.	D.	L.	F.	A.	Pts
38	28	4	6	74	36	60

1921-22 Division Two

After narrowly avoiding relegation in the two seasons after the First World War, Forest virtually ran away with the Second Division championship. Noah Burton was signed on a permanent basis and only missed one game but the real master-stroke came in the signing of former Liverpool, Aston Villa and England goalkeeper Sam Hardy, who was coaxed out of retirement. He conceded just 24 goals in his 32 appearances. After losing the opening game of the season 4-1 at Crystal Palace, Forest won their next seven matches. The club's top scorer was Jack Spaven with 18 goals.

P.	W.	D.	L.	F.	A.	Pts
42	22	12	8	51	30	56

1950-51 Division Three (South)

After being relegated to the Third Division (South) for the first time in their history in 1949, the club came close to winning promotion the following season but in 1950-51 they sprinted away with the title. They lost just one of their opening 19 games and set new divisional records for points (70) and goals scored (110). They beat Gillingham 9-2 and Aldershot 7-0 at the City Ground and won 6-1 against Crystal Palace at Selhurst Park. Wally Ardron broke Dave Martin's club goalscoring record with 36 goals whilst Tommy Capel weighed in with 23, including four goals in the victory over Gillingham.

P.	W.	D.	L.	F.	A.	Pts
46	30	10	6	110	40	70

1977-78 Division One

After finishing third in the Second Division and winning promotion in 1976-77, Brian Clough's side took the First Division by storm. He had already signed Birmingham's Kenny Burns to replace Bob Chapman who had moved to Notts County and early in the season signed Peter Shilton from Stoke City and Archie Gemmill from Derby County.

Forest won 11 of their first 16 games. After losing for only the third time on 19 November, 1-0 at Leeds United, the Reds went 26 games without defeat to finish as champions with 64 points, even more than runners-up Liverpool. Peter Withe and John Robertson finished as joint top scorers with 12 goals apiece.

P.	W.	D.	L.	F.	A.	Pts
42	25	14	3	69	24	64

1997-98 First Division

Nottingham Forest became First Division champions last season thus returning to the top flight after just one season outside the Premier League. The club's leading goalscorer was Pierre Van Hooijdonk with 29 league goals including hat-tricks against Queen's Park Rangers (Home 4-0) and Charlton Athletic (Home 5-2). He was also joint top scorer in the First Division and formed a deadly striking partnership with Kevin Campbell who scored 23 goals.

P.	W.	D.	L.	F.	A.	Pts
46	28	10	8	82	42	94

CHAPMAN, SAMMY

Joining Forest from Walsall junior football in 1962, the Wednesbury-born defender signed professional forms a year later and made his debut in a goalless draw at home to Stoke City on 18 January 1964.

Sammy Chapman

When he arrived at the City Ground he was regarded as a forward but after moving back into defence during an injury crisis, he then held down a regular place at centre-half. Appointed club captain, he was a strong, purposeful player who went on to play in 422 League and Cup games for the Reds before moving across the River Trent to join Notts County after Forest had signed Kenny Burns.

He went on to make 42 League appearances for the Meadow Lane club before ending his career with Shrewsbury Town.

CHARITY SHIELD

Nottingham Forest have appeared in two Charity Shield games. On 18 August 1959 they lost 3-1 to Wolverhampton Wanderers at Molineux with Tom Wilson netting for Forest. On 12 August 1978 they played Ipswich Town at Wembley and won 5-0 with goals from O'Neill (2), Withe, Lloyd and Robertson.

CHETTLE, STEVE

Steve Chettle came off the substitute's bench to make his Football League debut in a 4-3 defeat at Chelsea on 5 September 1987 and by the end of that season, he had been given a lengthy run in the right-back position. He retained this position until December 1988 when Brian Laws replaced him. He then moved to central defence and along with Terry Wilson shared the honour of partnering Des Walker. He won League Cup winners' medals against Luton Town in 1989 and Oldham Athletic the following year and by 1990-91 was a regular, missing just one game.

His position seemed at risk when Forest signed Carl Tiler but he fought his way back to be an ever-present in 1993-94 and miss just one game in each of the next two seasons. A loyal servant to the Forest club, he has appeared in 370 League games at the time of writing.

CITY GROUND

In 1898 after winning the FA Cup at Crystal Palace, Forest made their final move across the River Trent to their present ground, leaving the Town Ground in the city of Nottingham for the City Ground in West Bridgford.

Despite their Cup triumph, Forest still needed to raise an extra £3,000 to prepare the new ground and so they invited supporters and local businessmen to buy bonds worth £5 each.

A committee member by the name of William Bardill ordered the digging of a 'cellar' that ran the full length and breadth of the pitch, thus ensuring perfect drainage, which of course was vital with the ground being so close to the River Trent.

The City Ground remained unchanged for many years. The war too left Forest relatively unscathed with bombs causing just £75 worth of damage to the pitch in May 1941. There was a blow in the winter months of 1947 when the River Trent burst its banks and flooded the ground as high as the crossbars.

The first major ground improvements came in the 1950s with plans to build a stand at the Trent End of the ground but this was aborted in favour of the replacement of the derelict Main Stand. In 1958 a new stand was built on the East Side, providing an extra 2,500 seats. Forest were also the second but last top flight club to install floodlights, used first in September 1961 for the League Cup match with Gillingham which Forest won 4-1. In 1962 a new Main Stand was built with a cantilever roof providing cover for both seated spectators and those standing in the front of the enclosure.

On 24 August 1968 during a game against Leeds United, the Main Stand caught fire but fortunately no-one was injured. The next altercation in the appearance of the ground came in the summer of 1980 with the erection of the Executive Stand. Costing £2.5 million it closely resembled a stand erected at Molineux with a long angled cantilever with two tiers of seating divided by a line of executive boxes, giving a wonderful view of the pitch.

In 1990, Forrest chairman Maurice Roworth announced plans to develop all sides of the ground except the Executive Stand. Now with redevelopment of the ground completed, Nottingham Forest have an all-seater capacity of 30,602 with the City Ground being among the best in the country.

CLARK, FRANK

After breaking his leg early in his career, Frank Clark fought back to win almost every honour in the game except international recognition. He appeared at Wembley at the age of 19 when he played in Crook Town's 4-0 FA Amateur Cup Final replay win over Hounslow Town. Later moving to St James' Park, he was an ever-present in Newcastle's Second Division championship season of 1964-65 and also played in the Magpies FA Cup Final defeat against Liverpool in 1974. Moving to the City Ground in July 1975, he won plenty of honours with Forest including three League Cup medals and a European Cup winners' medal against Malmo.

After playing in 117 League games for the Reds, he entered management with Orient. After relegation in 1984-85, he twice led the O's to within reach of the play-offs before they won promotion in 1988-89 via the play-offs. In November 1986, Clark became a managing director and was given a seat on the board.

Frank Clark

He was the man given the difficult job of filling Brian Clough's shoes. After a disappointing start, his Forest side finished the 1993-94 season as runners-up to Crystal Palace to gain promotion to the Premier League. In 1994-95 Frank Clark's side finished third, only 10 points behind champions Blackburn Rovers and gained a UEFA Cup place.

In December 1996 with Forest languishing at the foot of the Premier League, Clark resigned his post. He was appointed manager of Manchester City but was dismissed as the Maine Road club headed for Second Division football.

CLEAN SHEET

This is the colloquial expression to describe a goalkeeper's perform-ance when he does not concede a goal. In the Football League, Peter Shilton kept 23 clean sheets in 37 appearances when Forest won the First Division championship in 1977-78. Playing in the other five games that season, John Middleton kept two clean sheets. The follow-ing season, Shilton kept 19 clean sheets from a full 42-match pro-gramme as Forest finished as runners-up. This equalled the record set by Harry Walker in 1950-51 when Forest won the Third Division (South) championship.

CLOUGH, BRIAN

One of nine children, Brian Clough worked as a clerk with ICI whilst playing for Billingham Synthonia and Great Broughton before joining Middlesborough. He was one of the greatest of marksmen with 204 goals in 222 appearances for 'Boro before moving to Sunderland in July 1961 for a fee of £45,000. Clough was the leading scorer in the Second Division for three seasons on the trot and scored 40 goals or more every season from 1956 to 1960.

He scored 63 goals in 74 appearances for Sunderland before an in-jury received against Bury on Boxing Day 1962 virtually ended his playing career. He tried to make a comeback but when he realised it was a hopeless cause, he retired from playing. He failed to score in ei-ther of his two internationals for England but would probably have won many more caps playing for a more fashionable southern club.

After a spell on Sunderland's coaching staff, he took his first steps in management with Hartlepool United, where a friend from his days at Middlesborough, Peter Taylor, joined him. He turned the club's fortunes around, building a squad that was to gain promotion at the end of the 1967-68 season. But by then, Clough and Taylor had moved to Derby County who were then a modest Second Division side. They made three major signings in Alan Hinton, Roy McFarland and John O'Hare before storming to the Second Division champion-ship. More major signings were made including Archie Gemmill, David Nish and Colin Todd and in

1971-72 the Rams won the League Championship for the first time in their history. The following season, Derby reached the semi-finals of the European Cup before losing to Juventus.

In October 1973, Clough shocked the football world by resigning as manager of Derby County following a dispute with Rams' chairman Sam Longson over his high-media profile. The players threatened to go on strike if he was not reinstated and the Derby fans held a series of public meetings in a bid to have their favourite restored. But it was all to no avail and the following month, he and Taylor accepted an offer to manage Third Division Brighton.

Clough left the south coast club in July 1974 and took over at Leeds United the following month. He arrived at Elland Road as the man to replace the much-respected Don Revie, who had become England manager. He was soon making major changes and there were rumours of an unhappy dressing-room atmosphere. The press blamed 'player power' when Clough was sacked after only 44 days in charge.

He was not out of work for long though and became the manager of Nottingham Forest in January 1975. Over the next 18 years he was to produce some golden moments for the Reds, including a League Championship, four League Cup wins and two European Cup successes. He persuaded Peter Taylor to leave Brighton and team up with him again. Sadly they fell out in 1982 and apparently never spoke to each other again before Taylor's death in 1990.

Forrest won promotion to the First Division in 1977 and a year later clinched the League title as they took the First Division by storm. Clough's skill in the transfer market in enticing Shilton, Burns, Gemmill and Dave Needham was the key to this success. In 1979 they beat Malmo thanks to a Trevor Francis goal. Clough had been the first British manager to spend a million pounds on one player when he signed Francis. A year later they confounded the critics when they won the European Trophy a second time. The Reds also played in six League Cup Finals between 1978 and 1992, winning four of them. He did not have too much success in the FA Cup until 1991 when they reached the final, only to lose to Spurs.

Brian Clough was never offered the England job, as his views were far too outspoken for the FA. He was offered the Welsh national team manager's job but Forest would not release him to carry out his duties on a part-time basis.

There is no doubt that Brian Clough is one of the greatest managers of all time, despite Forest's poor performances in 1992-93 when they fell to the foot of the new Premier League. Brian Clough decided to retire in May 1993 amidst a lot of bad publicity, having won just about everything there is to win.

CLOUGH, NIGEL

The son of former Forest manager Brian Clough, he was playing for Derby Sunday League side, AC Hunters when he signed professional forms for the Reds. He made his Forest debut on Boxing Day 1984 in a 2-0 home win over Ipswich Town. By the end of that season, he had gained a regular place in the Forest side. An ever-present in seasons 1986-87, 1989-90 and 1992-93, he soon made a name for himself as a creative player with excellent passing ability. However, he was also a prolific scorer, topping the club's goalscoring charts in six of the full eight seasons he was at the City Ground. He scored two hat-tricks for Forest - Queen's Park Rangers (Home 4-0 on 13 December 1987) and

Nigel Clough

Coventry City in the League Cup (Away 4-5 on 28 November 1990).

He made the first of his 14 England appearances whilst with Forest against Chile at the end of the 1988-89 season, the year that was without doubt his best for the club.

Before the start of the 1993-94 season, he left the City Ground to join Liverpool for a fee of £2.275 million. Hampered by injuries at Anfield he made just 44 first team appearances before moving to Manchester City in January 1996. Whilst at Maine Road he returned to the City Ground on loan and took his total of goals for the Reds to 131 in 412 first team appearances.

COLLINDRIDGE, COLIN

Entering the game late due to the Second World War, Colin Collindridge failed to impress the Forest officials in a trial at the City Ground and so in 1946 joined Sheffield United. He soon made a name for himself at Bramall Lane as a left-winger and in four seasons with the Blades, he scored 52 goals in 142 League appearances.

Forest manager Billy Walker snapped up the Kent-born winger just before the start of the club's 1950-51 promotion season. Making his debut in the opening game of the season, he scored one of the goals in Forest's 2-0 win at Newport County. He was an ever-present that season, scoring 18 League and Cup goals.

A great favourite with the City Ground crowd, he possessed terrific speed and a powerful shot and during his time with the club was the side's penalty taker.

He left Forest at the end of the 1953-54 season after scoring 47 goals in his 156 League and Cup appearances when he and his left-wing partner Tommy Capel signed for Coventry City in a double deal. He later ended his playing days with non-League Bath City.

COLLYMORE, STAN

A trainee at both Walsall and Wolverhampton Wanderers, he stayed on at Molineux as a non-contract player, while manage Graham Turner pondered over offering him a full contract. Finally released, he joined neighbouring Stafford Rangers and in 1990-91 he scored eight goals in ten consecutive games, prompting Crystal Palace to pay £100,000 for his services.

Only used as a substitute in his first season as a Palace player, he made his League debut at home to Queen's Park Rangers on 16 February 1991. It was another 13 months before he made his full League debut. He moved to Southend United and scored 15 goals in 30 League games before joining Forest.

In his first season at the City Ground, 1993-94, he was the club's top scorer with 19 goals and again in 1994-95 when he scored 22 goals in

37 games. Collymore had scored 45 goals in 78 first team games for the City Ground club when in July 1995 he moved to Liverpool for £8.5 million, the club's record transfer fee received.

Despite being in and out of the Liverpool side, he was a great favourite with the Anfield crowd and scored 35 goals in 81 first team outings before joining Aston Villa for £7 million in the summer of 1997.

Stan Collymore

COLOURS

Forest adopted red as the club colour from the outset after a set of red flannel caps was purchased for the players. They were known as the Garibaldi Reds after Guiseppe Garibaldi, one of the great men of the 19th century who achieved legendary status throughout Europe with his Red Shirt guerrilla army that helped unify Italy.

CONSECUTIVE HOME GAMES

In 1968-69, Forest were involved in an intense sequence of six home games in succession in the First Division. After losing 3-1 at Burnley on 1 March 1969 they were involved in the following list of matches at the City Ground before visiting Manchester United on 5 April, where they lost 3-1.

Date	Opponents	Score
04.03.1969	Queen's Park Rangers	1-0
08.03.1969	West Ham United	0-1
11.03.1969	Southampton	1-0
22.03.1969	West Bromwich Albion	3-0
24.03.1969	Manchester City	1-0
31.03.1969	Manchester United	0-1

CONSECUTIVE SCORING – LONGEST SEQUENCE

Grenville Morris and Dave 'Boy' Martin hold the club record for consecutive scoring when they were on target in eight consecutive League games. Morris' first came in the 2-1 defeat at Liverpool on 20 December 1902 and ended with his eleventh goal in that sequence as Forest drew 2-2 at Blackburn on 31 January 1903.

The first of Dave Martin's goals came in a 5-3 win over Fulham on 5 September 1936 and ended with his ninth and tenth goals in the sequence as Forest drew 2-2 at home to Chesterfield on 10 October.

CRICKETERS

Nottingham Forest have had six players who have also represented the county at cricket.

Sam Widdowson was a 'football legend'. Playing his first game for Forest in 1869, he remained a regular first-team player until his retirement in 1885. He played county cricket in 1878, scoring 15 runs in his two innings for Nottinghamshire.

William Gunn scored 18,295 runs for the county at an average of 34.07 and a highest score of 236 not out against Surrey at The Oval in 1898. He appeared in just one FA Cup match for Forest when they lost 4-1 to Aston Villa on Bonfire Day 1881. Whilst he played for Notts County he won two England caps.

Tinsley Lindley played cricket for Cambridge University though he wasn't awarded his Blue and Nottinghamshire and in 1888, he scored 64 runs at 10.67. He played in 25 FA Cup games for Forest, scoring 15 goals.

Making his debut for Nottinghamshire in 1899, Jim Iremonger was an outstanding cricketer. He scored 16,110 first-class runs with a top score of 272 against Kent in 1904 and took 696 wickets with a best of six for 7 against Essex at Trent Bridge in 1910. He toured Australia with the MCC in 1911-12 and was coach at Trent Bridge from 1921 to 1938. As a footballer he played in 300 League and Cup games for Forest.

Joe Hardstaff senior played in 12 first team games for the Reds scoring in the 4-0 win over Bolton Wanderers on 24 March 1906. He appeared in five Tests for England and scored 15,059 runs for

Nottinghamshire at an average of 30.75 and a top score of 213 against Sussex at Hove in 1913.

Walter Keeton also played Test cricket for England and scored 23,744 runs for Nottinghamshire at 40.18 and holds the record for the county's highest individual score, 312 not out against Middlesex in 1939. An inside-right with a powerful shot, he made five appearances for the Reds in the 1932-33 season.

CROSSLEY, MARK

Joining Forest straight from school, Mark Crossley made his League debut for the Reds as a replacement for the injured Steve Sutton in a 2-1 win at home to Liverpool on 26 October 1988. Three days later he kept a clean sheet in a 1-0 win over Newcastle United and although he had two short spells in the side the following term, deputising for Sutton, it wasn't until 1990-91 that he claimed a regular place, playing in every game.

He had a good game in the 1991 FA Cup Final against Tottenham Hotspur which Forest lost 2-1, saving a Gary Lineker penalty.

He started the following season as the first choice 'keeper before losing his place to Andy Marriott in March 1992 following a well publicised off the field incident in his home town.

Restored to favour by the end of the season, he was virtually an ever-present until the end of the 1996-97 season. Despite losing his place to Dave Beasant in 1997-98, the Welsh international 'keeper has appeared in 355 first team games for the City Ground club.

CROWD TROUBLE

However unwelcome, crowd disturbances are far from a modern phenomenon at major football matches. Behaviour at the City Ground has usually been of a high standard and though Forest supporters are well-renowned for voicing their opinions at suspect referees, the occasions when their demonstrations boil over beyond the verbal are very rare indeed.

Forest were indeed the victims of crowd trouble on 9 March 1974 when they played Newcastle United at St James' Park in the sixth round of the FA Cup. The match turned out to be one of the most controversial in the competition's history. Forest were leading 2-1 when they were awarded a second-half penalty. A Newcastle player was sent-off for protesting and after George Lyall had converted the kick, the referee had to take the players off as the Newcastle fans invaded the pitch. The game resumed after an eight-minute break and Newcastle with Forest shaken, scored three times to make it 4-3.

Forest appealed to the FA over the pitch invasion and the match was annulled and replayed at Goodison Park nine days later. That match was goalless but the Magpies won the third match 1-0 when the teams returned to Goodison Park three days later.

D

DARWEN

They joined the League when it was extended to 14 clubs in 1891-92 but finished bottom of the table and conceded 112 goals in 26 games. They were in the new Second Division the following season and won promotion at the first attempt but were immediately relegated.

The two clubs only met in season 1893-94 with Forest completing the 'double' over their Lancashire opponents. The Reds won the first meeting at Darwen 4-0 with Higgins (2) Collins and Brodie the scorers. The same players, along with Tom McInnes all scored in the 4-1 home win later in the season.

Darwen stayed in the Second Division until 1898-99 when they finished bottom of the table and conceded a League record 141 goals. They failed to gain re-election.

DAVENPORT, PETER

Born in Birkenhead, Peter Davenport began his footballing career as an amateur with Everton but in 1980 he was released. He first attracted Forest's attention when he was playing for Cammel Laird FC and in January 1982 he signed for the Reds. He made a sensational start to his Forest career, scoring four goals in his five appearances at the end of the 1981-82 season including a hat-trick in a 3-1 win at Ipswich Town.

He was hampered by injuries the following year but soon became Forest's number one striker, topping the club's scoring charts for the

Peter Davenport

next two seasons. In 1984-85 he hit his second hat-trick for the club in the 3-1 win over Sunderland on 1 September and won an England cap against the Republic of Ireland.

He scored his third hat-trick for Forest in 1985-86 in the 3-2 win over Arsenal but in March that season, he moved to Manchester United for £570,000. The move didn't work out for him and two years later he moved to Middlesborough for £700,000. In 1990-91 he was back in the top flight with Sunderland but after scoring 15 goals in 99 appearances, he moved on to Airdrie, St Johnstone and Stockport County.

DEBUTS

The only player to score a hat-trick on his debut for the club was James Collins, who scored three goals in Forest's 7-1 win at home to Wolverhampton Wanderers on the opening day of the 1893-94 season.

A number of players have scored two goals on their debut for the club, the most recent being Bert Bowery on 27 December 1975 in the 4-1 win against Blackburn Rovers at Ewood Park.

A debut with a difference was goalkeeper Peter Grummitt's who first appeared for the Reds in a 2-2 draw with Bolton Wanderers at the City Ground. He was beaten by a Jim Iley own-goal before he had even had the chance to touch the ball!

DEFEATS

Individual Games

Forest's worst home defeat in a first-class match was the 7-1 scoreline inflicted on the club by Birmingham City on 7 March 1959. Away from home the club's heaviest defeat was 9-1 at Ewood Park, Blackburn on 10 April 1937. The club also conceded nine goals at White Hart Lane on 29 September 1962 as Spurs ran out 9-2 winners.

Over a Single Season

Forest's worst defensive record in terms of defeats suffered in a single season was in 1971-72 when the club lost 25 of their 42 First Division matches and were relegated. Conversely, Forest only lost three matches in season's 1977-78 and 1978-79 when they finished first and second in the First Division respectively.

Consecutive League Matches with defeat

Forest's best run of League games without defeat is 42 and was established largely in season 1977-78. The run began on 26 November 1977 with a goalless draw at home to West Bromwich Albion and finished on 25 November 1978 with a 1-0 win over Bolton Wanderers at Burnden Park.

DEFENSIVE RECORDS

Nottingham Forest's best defensive record in the Football League was established in 1977-78 when the club won the First Division championship. Forest conceded just 24 goals in that campaign and were beaten in only three matches.

The club's worst defensive record in the Football League was in 1936-37 when they let in 90 goals in 42 matches to finish 18th in the Second Division.

DENT, JOHNNY

Spennymoor-born Johnny Dent played his early football with Spennymoor Rangers and Tudhoe United before moving into League football with Durham City in the Third Division (North) in 1923.

However, he was disillusioned with the League game and after just one season he left to join Tow Law Town. Some impressive performances for the non-League side led to him signing for Huddersfield Town in 1926 and though he played in three FA Cup semi-finals for the Terriers, he was not selected in the team that played Blackburn Rovers in 1928.

Forest signed him for £1,500 in October 1929 and he became an instant hit at centre-forward with the Reds' fans. He made his debut at home to Bradford and ended that season with 15 goals in 24 League games. Top goalscorer in seasons 1929-30, 1930-31 and 1933-34, he scored five hat-tricks - Rotherham United (Away 5-0 on 11 January

1930); Stoke City (Home 3-0 on 15 September 1930); Bradford (Home 6-1 on 23 January 1932); Oldham Athletic (Away 5-0 on 16 March 1935) and Burnley (Home 5-0 on 23 March 1935).

Making the best use of his powerfully-built frame, he scored 122 League and Cup goals in just 206 appearances for Forest before leaving the City Ground in 1936 to play for Kidderminster.

DEXTER, ARTHUR

After keeping goal for both Highbury Vale and Vernon Athletic in the Nottinghamshire Amateur Football League, he joined Stapleford Brookhill where his performances impressed the Forest club.

Signed in 1923, he made his Forest debut in the 1-0 home win over Everton in September of that year but then spent the next three seasons in the Reserves as understudy to Alfred Bennett and Len Langford, eventually replacing the latter when he moved to Manchester City in 1929.

Over the next four seasons, he only missed four games but then had to fight for the first team jersey with Percy Ashton, following his arrival from Melton Excelsior. After making the last of his 274 League and Cup appearances for Forest in 1937, he left the City Ground after the club had signed Allan Todd from Port Vale.

DICKINSON, BILLY

Joining his home-town club, Wigan Borough in 1924, the bustling forward was leading scorer for the Lancashire side for three consecutive seasons. His impressive performances for Wigan Borough led to a host of clubs wanting his services but it was Forest who signed him in 1928.

Making his debut on 15 September that year, he scored twice in Forest's 5-3 win over Swansea Town. Finding it difficult to break into the Forest side, he had to wait until the 1931-32 season before he won a regular place, forming a deadly partnership with Johnny Dent. He was the club's top scorer that season with 21 League goals.

He made 143 League and Cup appearances for Forest, scoring 73 goals, when he lost his place to Tom Peacock and left the club at the end of the 1933-34 season.

DISMISSALS

Nottingham Forest lasted longer than any other Football League club in not having a player sent off in the competition during the post-war period. But at the same time they had other players dismissed in other competitions. Moreover, Sammy Chapman had been dismissed playing for Forest's 'A' team, the Reserves and the first team in a cup-tie!

Gary Charles was the first Nottingham Forest player to be dismissed in the Premier League when he received his marching orders during the Reds game with Blackburn Rovers on 7 April 1993

DRAWS

Nottingham Forest played their greatest number of drawn League matches in a single season – 18 – in the 1969-70 season, when they finished 15th in the First Division, and 1978-79 when they finished as runners-up to Liverpool. The club drew their fewest number of matches – 3 – in the 1895-96 season when they ended the campaign 13th in the First Division.

The club's highest scoring draw is 4-4 when they played West Bromwich Albion at the City Ground on 28 October 1961.

The greatest number of drawn matches in a single Nottingham Forest cup-tie is three. This happened in three ties - Sheffield United (1922-23), West Bromwich Albion (1972-73) and Fulham (1974-75).

DUDLEY, WALTER

Rotherham-born Walter Dudley moved to Nottingham at a very early age. During his younger years he played at left-half and it was in this position that he made his Forest debut on 27 December 1902 in a 2-2 draw at home to Sheffield United. It was his only appearance that season and he had to wait until 5 March 1904 for his next!

The following season he broke into the first team at the expense of Jim Iremonger at left-back and began to play on a regular basis. After the emergence of Ginger Maltby, he switched to right-back and formed an effective full-back partnership that served Forest for over seven years.

A player with great positional sense and intelligence, he played the last of his 300 League and Cup games for Forest against Leeds City on 29 November 1913 when Forest went down 8-0.

E

EARLY GROUNDS

After taking its name from the Forest Recreation Ground on which its early years were spent, the club moved five times in the 33 years before it settled at the City Ground.

In 1879, Forest moved to a ground called The Meadows, which for several seasons had been the home of Notts County. A year later, Forest moved on to the most famous sporting venue in the town, Trent Bridge Cricket Ground. They would probably have stayed here longer than they did but in 1883, rivals Notts County moved in. They were to remain at Trent Bridge until 1910 when they moved across the river to a new ground on Meadow Lane.

Forest's next move took them to Park Side, Lenton to a ground, which cost them £300 to prepare. In 1885 they moved to Gregory Ground close to the Cottesmore School. The construction of the ground cost the club £500 and though spectators appeared to have been pleased with the new enclosure, the press bemoaned the fact that no provision had been made for them!

So in 1890, Forest returned to the Trent Bridge area to a place known as Woodward's Field, adjacent to the Town Arms near the junction of Arkwright Street and the Embankment. This new home, the Town Ground cost £1,000 and was scheduled to be opened for the first time on 3 October 1890 with a match arranged against Wolverhampton Wanderers. Notts County had a League match against Bolton Wanderers at Trent Bridge on the same day and complained to the Football League about the fixture clash.

The League refused permission for Wolves to play and so Forest played Scottish club Queen's Park instead, winning 4-1 in front of around 3,000 spectators. The Town Ground was Forest's first proper football stadium and it was here that the club staged the first official match using goalnets, when representative teams from the north and south played in 1891. Seven years later, Forest made their final move across the Trent to their present ground. The Town Ground became a tram depot and is still used by the local transport department.

EUROPEAN CUP

Nottingham Forest have participated in Europe's premier competition on three occasions. Their first opponents in the European Cup were Liverpool and Forest confirmed their position as the best side in the country with a 2-0 aggregate win. There followed victories over AEK Athens, Grasshoppers and Cologne to reach the final. The semi-final meetings with Cologne proved to be the club's biggest test. They looked to have destroyed the Reds European dream after drawing 3-3 at the City Ground but Ian Bowyer hit the goal in Germany to make it a night of glory.

Swedish club Malmo were Forest's opponents in the 1979 European Cup Final in Munich. Trevor Francis in his first European game stretched himself at the far post for a spectacular winner in a disappointing final, which was continuing the trend of matches being decided by a single goal. John McGovern lifted the huge trophy - Nottingham Forest had been crowned Kings of Europe.

Forest retained the trophy the following year. After beating Osters IF and Arges Pitesti in the first two rounds, the Reds were severely tested by Dynamo Berlin in the quarter-final. The East Germans won 1-0 at the City Ground but two goals by a Francis and a John Robertson penalty proved more than enough as Forest won the away leg 3-1. Francis and another Robertson penalty gave them a two-goal lead against Ajax in the semi-final and although the Dutch pulled a goal back on their own soil, they could not force extra-time.

Their opponents in the Madrid final were Hamburg with Kevin Keegan in their ranks. John Robertson with a right foot shot from just outside the penalty area scored the only goal. However, the real hero was Peter Shilton who pulled off a string of fine saves.

The Reds lost their grip on the European Cup in the first round in 1980-81 when CSKA Sofia beat them 1-0 twice.

EUROPEAN SUPER CUP

Barcelona were defeated 2-1 on aggregate in the European Super Cup with Forest's goal in their 1-0 win at the City Ground being scored by Charlie George, who enjoyed a brief loan spell at the club. The following season, Valencia beat Forest on the away-goals rule after two Ian Bowyer goals had given the Reds a 2-1 win at the City Ground.

EVER-PRESENTS

There have been 53 Nottingham Forest players who have been ever-present throughout a Football League season. The greatest number of ever-present seasons by a Forest player is eight by Bobby McKinlay. The full list is:

No of Seasons	Players
8	Bobby McKinlay
4	George Needham
3	Jack Armstrong; Nigel Clough; Jim Iremonger; Henry Newton; Archie Ritchie; John Robertson;
2	Jack Burkitt; Frank Clark; Mark Crossley; Walter Dudley; Peter Grummitt; Peter Hindley; Harry Linacre; Tom McInnes; Billy McKinlay; Liam O'Kane; Peter Shilton; Harry Walker; Bob Wallace; John Winfield;
1	Dennis Allsop; Percy Barratt; Jimmy Barrington; Jim Barron; Garry Birtles; Ian Bowyer; Harry Bulling; Noah Burton; Jack Calvey; Arthur Capes; Sammy Chapman; Jack Coleman; Colin Collindridge; Dan Edgar; Horace Gager; Steve Hodge; Edwin Hughes; Brian Laws; Larry Lloyd; Ginger Maltby; Alan Moore; Gerry Morgan; Bill Morley; Alan Rogers; Adam Scott; Fred Scott; Jack Spaven; Geoff Thomas; Des Walker; Neil Webb; Bill Whare;

F

FA CUP

Nottingham Forest first entered the FA Cup in November 1878, beating Notts at home 3-1. They later beat Sheffield 2-0 and Oxford University 2-1 before losing at the semi-final stage to Old Etonians 2-1. In the 1879-80 FA Cup fourth round, Nottingham Forest and Sheffield drew 2-2 but Sheffield were disqualified for refusing to play extra-time! More FA Cup success followed as Forest fell at the semi-final stage twice in five years. During these years Forest recorded their highest victory, winning 14-0 at Clapton in a first round tie.

The Reds reached their first FA Cup Final in 1898 but their route to the tie was packed with incident. After two 4-0 wins over Grimsby

Town and Gainsborough Trinity, both Second Division sides, Forest beat West Bromwich Albion 3-2 in the quarter-finals after being 2-1 down at half-time. Facing Southampton, the Southern League champions in the semi-final at Bramall Lane, the Reds drew 1-1 and so a replay was necessary. Two last-minute goals from Tom McInnes and Chas Richards were enough to take Forest into the final. The Saints protested fiercely after the replay was held up by a snowstorm, claiming that the game should never have been restarted. In the final, Forest met Derby County at the Crystal Palace and won 3-1 thanks to two goals by Arthur Capes and a third by captain John MacPherson minutes from time.

Nottingham Forest have been drawn to play FA Cup games in all four home countries. In 1885 they drew their semi-final with Queen's Park at Derby and then lost the replay in Edinburgh 3-0. In 1888-89 they were drawn to play Linfield in Belfast only to discover on arrival that their opponents had scratched. However, they did play a friendly and were beaten 3-1. In 1921-22 they lost 4-1 away to Cardiff City.

They reached their second Cup Final in 1959 when quite remarkably, the same eleven players represented the club throughout the nine-match run including the final itself. In round three, non-League Tooting and Mitcham led 2-0 with just 38 minutes to play before Forest fought back to force a draw and win the replay. Grimsby were beaten 4-1 before three games were needed to account for Birmingham City with Roy Dwight hitting a hat-trick in a 5-0 second replay win. Two goals from Tommy Wilson gave Forest a 2-1 sixth round win over Bolton Wanderers before a Johnny Quigley goal gave Forest victory in the semi-final against Aston Villa. In the final against Luton Town, goals from Dwight, who was later stretchered off and Wilson, gave Forest a 2-1 victory.

Forest reached the semi-final stage again in 1967, defeating cup holders Everton 3-2 in the sixth round with Storey-Moore scoring a hat-trick. Unfortunately they went down 2-1 to Spurs with Terry Hennessey netting for Forest.

In 1987-88 Forest reached the semi-final stage again even though they were not once drawn at home. A 4-1 win at Halifax was followed by a 2-1 victory at Orient before a Gary Crosby goal was enough to defeat Birmingham City at St Andrew's. Goals from Paul Wilkinson and Brian Rice coupled with a superb display of goalkeeping by Steve

Sutton gave Forest a 2-1 win at Arsenal. Again Forest couldn't get past the semi-final stage, losing 2-1 to Liverpool.

Forest reached the semi-finals the season after without conceding a goal. Drawn yet again against Liverpool, the game was abandoned after only a few minutes following a crush of spectators at the Leppings Lane end of the Hillsborough ground and 95 people lost their lives. The rearranged semi-final took place 22 days later but Forest went down 3-1.

Just over a year later, Forest reached their first FA Cup Final for 32 years. A Stuart Pearce free-kick gave them a half-time lead but their opponents Spurs equalised and then won in extra-time through an unfortunate Des Walker own-goal.

FA CUP FINALS

1898: Nottingham Forest 3, Derby County 1

Having beaten Forest 5-0 at the Baseball Ground, Derby County entered the 1898 final as firm favourites even though the Reds had fielded a weakened side that day. Johnny MacPherson led out a Forest side showing five changes from the one beaten at Derby. Forest took a deserved lead after 19 minutes when Capes latched on to Billy Wragg's free-kick to shoot past Fryer in the Derby goal. This spurred the Rams into action and twelve minutes later, Steve Bloomer equalised. However, just before the interval, Capes scored his and Forest's second goal after Fryer had failed to hold a Sammy Richards shot.

In the second-half, Derby pressed forward and it seemed only a matter of time before they drew level. On one occasion, Forest 'keeper Allsop was beaten by a Bloomer shot only for MacPherson to block his short on the line. The Forest captain then put the matter beyond doubt by scoring Forest's third goal.

The Forest side was: Allsop; Ritchie; Scott; Forman; MacPherson; Wragg; McInnes; Richards; Benbow; Capes; Spouncer.

1959: Nottingham Forest 2, Luton Town 1

Forest overcame an even greater handicap 61 years later when they lost Roy Dwight with a broken leg. Forest's side was the one that had played in every round of the competition. The Reds took the lead after only eight minutes when Dwight converted an Imlach cross. Two minutes later Tommy Wilson headed over Luton 'keeper Baynham to put Forest 2-0 up. Just before half-time, Roy Dwight, the scorer of Forest's first goal was stretchered off with a broken leg and the Reds were down to ten men. Luton pulled a goal back through Dave Pacey but with Bobby McKinlay in outstanding form, Forest held on to their lead to win the cup for a second time.

The Forest side was: Thomson; Whare; McDonald; Whitefoot; McKinlay; Burkitt; Dwight; Quigley; Wilson; Gray; Imlach.

1991: Nottingham Forest 1, Tottenham Hotspur 2 (aet)

With Spurs striving for a record eighth win, Brian Clough kept faith with the side that had beaten West Ham in the semi-final. This meant that youngsters Gary Charles, Roy Keane and Lee Glover were given their chance ahead of the more experienced Brian Laws, Steve Hodge and Nigel Jemson. However, all eyes were on Paul Gascoigne who was supposedly playing his last game for Spurs before his £5 million transfer to Lazio.

Only two minutes had gone when Gascoigne's studs left an impression on the chest of Garry Parker and then the former Newcastle star brought down Charles with a nasty tackle. From the free-kick Stuart Pearce opened the scoring for Forest, hitting a magnificent shot through the Spurs defensive wall. Minutes later, Gascoigne was stretchered off, his knee ligaments damaged in his foul on Charles.

After 32 minutes, Spurs were awarded a penalty when Crossley brought down Gary Lineker. The Forest 'keeper dived to his left to beat out Lineker's penalty-kick and it looked all over for Spurs. However, in the second-half, Spurs' pressure told and after 54 minutes, Paul Stewart equalised. The game moved into extra-time and though Spurs always looked dangerous, their winning goal was a cruel way for Forest to lose. Nayim's corner was headed on by Stewart, only for Des Walker to beat Gary Mabbutt to the ball and head over Gary Charles on the line for Tottenham's winner.

The Forest side was: Crossley; Charles; Pearce; Walker; Chettle; Keane; Crosby; Parker; Clough; Glover (Laws); Woan (Hodge).

FATHER AND SON

Nottingham Forest have boasted a number of father and son relationships, perhaps the most notable being Brian Clough and his son Nigel. One of the greatest managers in the history of football, he brought seven major trophies to the City Ground during his 18 years in charge. Nigel Clough moved to Liverpool before the start of the 1993-94 season after finishing as the Reds top scorer in six out of the eight full seasons in which he was a member of the first team.

Archie Gemmill won a League Championship and League Cup winners' medal with Forest, appearing in 80 first team games before being allowed to join Birmingham City. His son Scot played his first game for the Reds on 6 April 1991 and at the time of writing has appeared in 222 League games for the City Ground club.

Sandy Higgins holds the club individual scoring record with five goals in one game, scored in the match against Clapton in January 1891. His son, also named Alexander played in 35 League games during the 1920-21 season.

Frank Hindley played in eight first team games before the war, but it was his son Peter who hit the headlines. Forming a solid full-back partnership with John Winfield, the Worksop-born defender played in 416 League and Cup games for the Reds.

One of Forest's most recent acquisitions is former Leeds United player Andy Gray. His father Frank, who also played for Leeds United, made 118 first team appearances for the Reds in two seasons at the City Ground.

FIRE

A fire broke out in the main stand at the City Ground during Forest's First Division match against Leeds United on 24 August 1968. The stand, which had only been completed some three years earlier was gutted. The match was abandoned but fortunately easy access to the safety of the playing area enabled spectators to escape without any serious injuries. In fact, several thousand watched the fire brigade in action instead of the players.

Forest borrowed Notts County's Meadow Lane ground for home matches but failed to win any of the six games played there.

FIRST DIVISION

Nottingham Forest were accepted by the Football League after its expansion in 1892 and though Alliance members were incorporated into a new Second Division, Forest and Sheffield Wednesday went straight into the First Division. The club's first opponents were Everton who had been champions in 1890 and a 2-2 draw was secured with Sandy Higgins scoring both Forest's goals.

During the early years of the twentieth century, the club started to slide down the League and in 1905-06 suffered relegation for the first time. After winning promotion the following season, Forest went down again in 1911 and did not return until 1922-23. After surviving relegation by the narrowest of margins in the next two seasons, they returned to the Second Division in 1925 after winning just six of their 42 matches.

After an absence of 32 years, Forest were back in the top flight for the 1957-58 season and though they topped the table in October, they ended the season in tenth place. After winning the FA Cup in 1958-59, great things were expected of Forest the following season, yet only a 3-0 win over Newcastle United in the penultimate match of the season saved them from relegation. There followed six seasons of mainly mid-table placings before in 1966-67 the club found a new level of consistency and in one run of 24 games just 15 goals were conceded. Forest finished the season as runners-up to Manchester United. There followed another four seasons of mediocre football before relegation finally came in 1972.

Promoted at the end of the 1976-77 season, Forest took the First Division by storm, winning 11 of their first 16 games. They went 26 games without defeat to finish as champions, seven points ahead of Liverpool. Retaining the League Championship was never going to be easy and it was made all the more difficult when they drew six of their first seven games. Nonetheless, Forest were up with the leading pack and didn't lose a game until the 17th match of the season at Anfield. They went through the rest of the season with just two defeats and finished as runners-up to Liverpool.

On 17 November 1979, Brighton became the first side in 52 matches to beat Forest at the City Ground when they won 1-0. A late revival that season lifted Forest to fifth. After finishing seventh in 1980-81, Forest slumped to twelfth the following campaign but 1982-83 was a better season as the Reds moved up to fifth. The club's improvement continued in 1983-84 and after a mixed start they finished third, six points off the top.

Though they headed the early tables in 1984-85 they lost form and finished ninth. In 1986-87, Forest won 11 of the first 18 matches and in December they stood in second place. However, their challenge fell away and they finished eighth, as they had the previous season. Another title challenge was mounted in 1987-88 but their hopes faded in the second half of the season and they finished third, 17 points adrift of champions Liverpool. In 1988-89 six victories in succession at the turn of the year enabled the Reds to once again finish in third place. There followed three disappointing seasons before Forest were relegated to the 'First Division' following reorganisation in 1992-93.

After a disappointing start, a 13-game unbeaten run pushed the Reds into promotion contention. Losing only one of their last 16 matches, Forest finished the season as runners-up to Crystal Palace. After being relegated from the Premier League in 1996-97, Forest won the First Division championship in 1997-98 with a record total of 94 points.

FIRST LEAGUE MATCH

Forest's first League match took place at Goodison Park on 3 September 1892, with their opponents being Everton who had been League champions in 1890. Not only was it Forest's first League match but it was also the first League match to be played at Everton's new Goodison Park stadium.

Both sides had early chances but it was Forest's Sandy Higgins who opened the scoring, fastening on to a long throw-in before shooting past Jardine in the Everton goal. The home side equalised against the run of play when Brown failed to hold Geary's shot which trickled over the line. This spurred Everton on but the Forest defence held firm and at half-time, there was no further score.

Everton took the lead with just ten minutes remaining when Maxwell crossed for left-winger Chadwick to easily beat Brown from close range. Letts, the Everton outside-right missed an easy chance to put the game beyond Forest's reach before McCallum and Pike set up a chance for Higgins. The Scotsman's downward header was fumbled by Everton 'keeper Jardine and the ball bounced into the net for the equaliser. Then with just 60 seconds remaining Forest almost snatched the winner when Higgins in search of his third goal sent in a shot which Jardine did well to tip round the post.

The Forest side was: Brown; Earp; Scott; Hamilton; A.Smith; McCracken; McCallum; W.Smith; Higgins; Pike; McInnes.

FIRST MATCH

Forest's first opponents were Notts County Football Club. The match took place on 26 March 1866. The match was billed as 'The Garibaldis' versus 'The Lambs' and took place on the Forest Recreation Ground. Forest's club history published in 1891 reports that Forest won 1-0 with Revis touching down the ball after a close race with County's Browne. The Daily Guardian however, published the morning after the match said that 'County's 11 men held on against Forest's 17 to register a no-score draw'. Unfortunately the truth will never be established as the make-up of the Forest side on that historic day was never recorded.

FLOOD

In the severe winter of 1946-47, heavy flooding left the City Ground totally submerged. In fact, swans from the River Trent glided along the full length of the pitch as water crept up to the height of the crossbars. The flood also swamped the club's offices and many of the official records were lost. Neighbours, Notts County allowed the Reds to share their Meadow Lane ground until the flood had subsided.

FLOODLIGHTS

Nottingham Forest were the second but last First Division club to install floodlights at their ground. They were first used on 11 September 1961 for a first round League Cup match against Gillingham. Forest won 4-1 in front of a 10,991 crowd with goals from Vowden (2), Booth and Addison.

FOOTBALL ALLIANCE

When the Football League was formed in 1888, Nottingham Forest were not included in the original membership of 12. The club sought regular football elsewhere, firstly joining the ill-fated Combination League and then the Football Alliance.

After finishing bottom in 1898-99 including losing 12-0 at Small Heath, Forest finished fourth the following season and applied to join the Football League. Though their application was initially rejected, they were accepted at the end of the 1891-92 season after becoming Alliance champions. Alliance members were incorporated into a new Second Division, although Forest and Sheffield Wednesday went straight into Division One.

FOOTBALL COMBINATION

Nottingham Forest reserves spent nine seasons in the Football Combination from 1958-59 to 1966-67 with a highest position of fourth in 1963-64.

FOOTBALLER OF THE YEAR

The Football Writers' Footballer of the Year award has only been won once by a Nottingham Forest player and that was in 1977-78 when Kenny Burns was the recipient. The Professional Football Association award for Player of the Year went to Peter Shilton, also in 1977-78. Forest's Tony Woodcock was voted Young Player of the Year in the same season.

FOOTBALL LEAGUE CUP

Nottingham Forest have won the Football League (later Milk, Littlewoods, Rumbelows and Coca Cola) Cup on four occasions and have also been losing finalists on two occasions.

Their first game in the competition was on 5 October 1960 when two goals from Bill Younger were enough to beat Halifax Town 2-0. For a time, Forest did not appear interested in the League Cup and at times even failed to participate during its early years. But once the final was booked for Wembley, their interest began to grow, although it took a few years before they finally lifted the trophy.

In 1977-78, Shilton, Gemmill and Needham were all cup-tied and so 18-year-old goalkeeper Chris Woods had to deputise for the England 'keeper. Forest beat West Ham 5-0 in the second round and then scored four goals against Notts County and Aston Villa to reach the quarter-finals where they beat Bury 3-0 at Gigg Lane. In the semi-final they met Leeds United. In the first leg at Elland Road, two goals from Peter Withe helped the Reds to a 3-1 win and though the Yorkshire side provided a few scares at the City Ground by going 2-1 up, Forest rallied to win 4-2 on the night and 7-3 on aggregate. Playing Liverpool in the Final, the game ended in a goalless stalemate but in the replay at Old Trafford, a John Robertson penalty was enough to secure the Reds their first major trophy in 19 seasons.

In 1978-79, a 3-1 aggregate win over Watford in the semi-final put Brian Clough's side into their second League Cup Final. This time the Reds did not require a replay as two goals by Birtles and another by Woodcock gave them a 3-2 win over Southampton.

In 1979-80, Forest reached the League Cup Final for the third successive season after squeezing past West Ham and Liverpool. However, a silly misunderstanding between Needham and Shilton enabled Wolves to take the trophy by a single Andy Gray goal. In reaching three consecutive finals, Forest went a record 25 League Cup matches without defeat.

Forest reached the Wembley Final for a fourth time in 1989 after dismissing Chester, Coventry, Leicester and Queen's Park Rangers (where Lee Chapman scored four goals in Forest's 5-2 win) and playing Bristol City in the semi-final. Paul Martdon gave the Ashton Gate

The victorious Forest side with the Football League Cup in 1979.

side a shock lead at the City Ground before a John Pender own goal levelled the scores. In the return leg at Ashton Gate, the Forest faithful had to endure 116 minutes of torrential rain before Garry Parker scored the only goal of the game. Forest's opponents at Wembley were their 1959 FA Cup Final opposition, Luton Town. Two goals from Nigel Clough and one from Neil Webb gave Forest a 3-1 win after the Hatters had taken the lead.

Forest returned to Wembley in 1990 where their opponents were Oldham Athletic. The Reds most notable result was a 3-2 win over Spurs at White Hart Lane in the fifth round. In the final, a single goal by Nigel Jemson was enough to beat the Boundary Park club and secure the club their fourth League Cup.

The Reds reached their sixth League Cup Final in 1992 only to lose by a single goal to Manchester United.

Forest's best scoreline in the competition was established on 23 September 1980 when the Reds beat Bury 7-0 at Gigg Lane. Stuart Pearce has made the most League Cup appearances with 60 whilst Nigel Clough is the club's leading scorer in the competition with 22 goals.

FOREIGN PLAYERS

Nottingham Forest have had a number of foreign-born players on their staff. During the summer of 1980, the club spent £400,000 on Swiss international Raimondo Ponte from Grasshoppers of Zurich and signed Norwegian international Einar Aas from Bayern Munich. Unfortunately, neither of them managed to produce the goods. The arrival of Jurgen Rober from Chicago the following season added little to the Forest cause.

In 1982-83 Dutch international goalkeeper Hans van Breukelen was signed to replace Peter Shilton. He in turn was replaced by Hans Segers, who later went on to serve Wimbledon. Another Dutchman to play for Forest was Frans Thijssen who was signed from Ipswich Town in 1983. Perhaps the most famous Dutchman to play for Forest was Johnny Metgod who joined the club from Real Madrid. The midfield maestro played in 139 League and Cup games for the Reds before signing for Tottenham Hotspur.

Another Norwegian international to play for Forest was Kjetll Osvold. Signed from Lillestrom, he only played in a handful of first-team games before going on loan to Leicester City. Icelandic international Toddy Orlygsson joined Forest in November 1989 and played in 37 League games before signing for Stoke City.

In 1993-94, Norwegian international Alf-Inge Haaland joined the Reds whilst the following season, the Reds signed midfielder Lars Bohinen who later left to play for Blackburn Rovers and Dutchman Bryan Roy who is the club's record signing. Andrea Silenzi joined the club from Torino but failed to impress the City Ground faithful. Other overseas players to have played for Forest include Nikola Jerkan who joined the club from Oviedo, Frenchman Thiery Bonalair, Italian goalkeeper Marco Pascolo, Norwegian Jon Olav Hjelde and Dutchman Pierre van Hooijdonk who was the club's leading scorer in 1997-98.

Forest have also had on their books some players who, though not born on foreign shores, had very foreign-sounding names – notably Dick Le Flem, David Serella, Justin Fashanu and Robert Rosario.

Hans van Breukelen

FORMAN, FRANK

Born in the South Derbyshire village of Aston-on-Trent, he played for the village team and Beeston United before signing for Derby County in March 1894. He was only at the Baseball Ground for nine months as the Rams failed to appreciate the youngster's vast potential.

Still only 19, he joined his brother Fred at Forest and within three years, had won the first of his nine England caps. Also that season he was a member of the Forest team that beat his former club Derby 3-1 in the FA Cup Final at Crystal Palace. The following year, Frank and Fred Forman were both capped at the same time, the last pair of brothers to play in the same England team until Bobby and Jack Charlton in 1965.

One of the best half-backs in the country, he replaced John MacPherson as captain when he left for Motherwell and continued to serve Forest until 1905 when he played his last game in a 2-1 win at Small Heath.

After retiring as a player, he joined the club's committee and was elected a life member.

FOUNDATION

One of the oldest football clubs in the world, Nottingham Forest was formed at a meeting in the Clinton Arms in 1865. Known originally as the Forest Football Club, the game which first drew the founders together was 'shinney' a form of hockey. When they determined to change to football in 1865, one of their first moves was to buy a set of red caps to wear on the field.

FRANCIS, TREVOR

Plymouth-born Trevor Francis made his name with Birmingham City in the early 1970s and in February 1971 he became the first 16-year-old to score four goals in a League game when City beat Bolton Wanderers 4-0. He played in two FA Cup semi-finals for the St Andrew's club and in February 1977 won the first of 52 caps for England against Holland.

After 280 League games for Birmingham City in which he scored 118 goals, he became Britain's first seven-figure signing when Forest paid a reported £1.5 million for his services in February 1979.

Trevor Francis, winner of 52 caps for England.

Though he was often plagued by injuries, there was never any doubt over his outstanding talent and goalscoring ability. It was Francis who scored the winning goal in the 1979 European Cup Final against FF Malmo. He only scored one hat-trick during his stay at the City Ground and that came in a 4-0 win over Manchester City on 23 February 1980.

It was Manchester City who signed Francis just one week into the 1981-82 season but a year later after scoring 12 goals in 26 League games he was on his way to Sampdoria for £700,000. He won an Italian Cup winners' medal with Sampdoria and later played for Atalanta before signing for Glasgow Rangers in 1988. A Skol Cup winners' medal at Ibrox Park was followed by a return to League football with Queen's Park Rangers. After spending a year as player-manager at Loftus Road he took up a similar position with Sheffield Wednesday but is now back at his beloved St Andrew's as Birmingham's manager.

G

GAGER, HORACE

London-born Horace Gager first came to the attention of Luton Town whilst playing for Vauxhall Motors but like so many players of his generation, he lost a major part of his career to the Second World War.

During the hostilities he 'guested' for Glentoran in the Northern Ireland Regional League along with former Forest favourite Dave 'Boy' Martin. Returning to Kenilworth Road after the war, he played in 59 League games for the Hatters before joining Forest in February 1948.

Making his first team debut in the 1-0 win over Leicester City at the end of that month, he was soon displaying his abilities as a centre-half.

Appointed Forest's club captain when Bob McCall dropped out of the first team in 1951, he made the last of his 268 appearances at the age of 37 in 1955.

GAINSBOROUGH TRINITY

They spent 16 seasons, all in the Second Division between 1896 and 1912 without ever managing to finish any higher than sixth. The two clubs met on four occasions with Forest winning all the encounters. Goals from Morris, Whitchurch and Shearman gave Forest a 3-2 away win in 1906-07 whilst Morris (2) and West scored in the Reds' 3-1 home win. The last season the clubs met was 1911-12, Trinity's last season in the Football League, the Reds winning 2-0 at the City Ground and 2-1 in Lincolnshire.

GEMMILL, ARCHIE

Born in Paisley, he began his football career with St Mirren in 1964 before joining Preston North End for £16,000 in June 1967. After three years at Deepdale he moved to Derby County for £60,000 and it was under Brian Clough's management that his career really began to take off. Bringing a competitive edge to every game, he played a significant role in helping the Rams to win the League title in 1972 and again in 1975.

Gemmill was a non-stop 90-minute competitor, at his best when running with the ball. This industrious side to Gemmill's talent obviously appealed to Clough, for when he was in charge of Forest in 1977-78, he went back to Derby to sign him.

He went straight into the Forest side at home to Norwich City in October 1977 and played in 34 games that season, finishing on the losing side only twice. At the end of the campaign he picked up his third League Championship medal. In 1978-79 he was instrumental in helping Forest to reach the European Cup Final. However, he didn't play on the big day, being on the substitute's bench as Forest beat Malmo 1-0 in Munich.

A valued member of the Scotland squad, he played 43 times at full level and no-one who ever saw his goal against Holland in the 1978 World Cup will forget it. He had already scored from the penalty spot to give the Scots a 2-1 lead when in the 68th minute of this vital qualifying match, he picked the ball up wide on the right. He threaded his way through the Dutch defence, evading three strong challenges before shooting home past the diving Jongblood.

In August 1979 he was allowed to leave Forest to join Birmingham City. He later played for Wigan Athletic before returning to the Baseball Ground for a second spell. He joined Forest's coaching staff in August 1985 and was re-registered as a player early the following year. He later shared the managerial duties at Rotherham United with former Forest colleague John McGovern.

Archie Gemmill

GIBSON, SYD

Joining Forest from Kettering Town in 1921, he made his League debut for the Reds on 22 October that year in a 1-0 defeat at West Ham United. Though he played at centre-forward in that match, it was at outside-right that he was to make a name for himself at the City Ground. Although not a prolific scorer, he topped the club's goalscoring charts in seasons 1925-26 and 1926-27, the latter being his best campaign when he hit 17 goals. A regular in the Forest side for seven seasons, there were many followers of the game who felt that if he had moved into a higher grade of football during this time, he would have won an international call-up.

After only five matches of the 1928-29 season, he was allowed to leave the City Ground after Forest refused to meet his wage demands and he joined Sheffield United for £5,000.

A popular player with the Bramall Lane club, he had to retire following a knee injury sustained in a match with Derby County in January 1932.

GILLIES, MATT

He was on wartime service with the RAF when he signed for Bolton Wanderers in October 1942, having previously been on Motherwell's books as an amateur. During the war he also 'guested' for Arsenal, Queen's Park Rangers and Chelsea. In January 1952 after 145 League appearances for the Trotters, he joined Leicester City for £10,000. He won a Second Division championship medal in 1953-54 but two years later retired from playing.

Appointed coach at Filbert Street, he later became caretaker manager and was given full managerial duties on a permanent basis in January 1959.

He led Leicester to two FA Cup Finals in 1961 and 1963 and a League Cup victory in 1964 when they beat Stoke City in a two-legged final. After breaking the British transfer record to sign Allan Clarke from Fulham for £150,000, he resigned in December 1968, shortly after first-team coach Bert Johnson had been sacked.

Two months later he was appointed manager of Nottingham Forest. However, over the next three and a half seasons he enjoyed little success. The Reds finished in the bottom half of the First Division in each of his terms in charge before being relegated in 1972.

After being booed by the fans and with the club struggling in the lower reaches, he tendered his resignation, much to the relief of the Forest fans.

GLOSSOP NORTH END

Glossop North End won promotion to the First Division at the end of their first season in the League, 1898-99. They were relegated the following season and spent the rest of the time in the lower division.

The two clubs first met on 16 September 1899 when North End won 3-0 on their home ground. Forest more than gained revenge in the return, beating their Derbyshire opponents 5-0 with goals from Calvey (2), MacPherson, Capes and Norris. The clubs did not meet again until 1906-07 when Forest won both matches 2-0. Season 1912-13 saw two entertaining games, Forest winning 3-2 at the City Ground and North End winning by the odd goal in a seven-goal thriller at Glossop. A John Coleman goal gave Forest the points the last time the clubs met on 6 March 1915. Glossop finished bottom of the League that season and resigned from the competition shortly before the resumption of matches in 1919.

GOALKEEPERS

Nottingham Forest have almost always been extremely well served by their goalkeepers and most of them have been highly popular with the supporters.

Dennis Allsop replaced Forest's first goalkeeper in the Football League, the erratic William Brown and won an FA Cup winners' medal in 1898 when he turned in an outstanding performance in Forest's 3-1 win over Derby County. Replacing Allsop was Harry Linacre, an outstanding 'keeper who won two England caps and a Second Division championship medal in 1907.

Brother of the famous Notts County goalkeeper Albert Iremonger, Jim Iremonger made a name for himself as a full-back before reverting to the role of custodian in 1907. He had the quietest afternoon of his career on 21 April 1909 as he watched the Forest forwards score 12 goals against Leicester Fosse. His brother Harry kept goal for the Reds between 1914 and 1915.

Following a distinguished career with Liverpool and Aston Villa, Sam Hardy 'guested' for the Reds during their Victory Shield success of 1919, before finally signing for the club in August 1921. He was instrumental in Forest's success that season as they won the Second Division championship, only conceding 23 goals in 32 games. The oldest player to represent the club, injury forced his retirement at the age of 41.

Up to the Second World War, the club were served by three goal-keepers in Len Langford, who was ever-present in 1926-27, Arthur Dexter who understudied Langford before playing in 274 first team games and Percy Ashton, a consistent if unspectacular 'keeper who despite playing in 185 games for Forest was prone to the odd mistake.

Forest signed an excellent 'keeper just after the war in Harry Walker. Nicknamed 'Mr Consistency' he was outstanding in Forest's Division Three (South) championship-winning season of 1950-51.

Peter Grummitt was Forest's first-choice 'keeper for nine years and was one of the best never to win a full cap. He had an outstanding season in 1966-67, helping Forest to the semi-final of the FA Cup and runners-up in the First Division, where he kept 13 clean sheets and conceded just 41 goals.

Chris Woods sprang to fame in 1977-78 when he played in every match from the third round to the final of the League Cup and kept two clean sheets as Forest beat Liverpool 1-0 after a goalless draw at Wembley. The following season he made his debut for the England Under-21s, being the first player to be selected without a League appearance to his name.

There is no doubt that Peter Shilton enjoyed the best years of his glittering career at the City Ground. He was selected as PFA Player of the Year in 1978 and won a League Championship medal, a League Cup winners' medal and two European Cup winners' medals.

Chris Woods

Steve Sutton turned in some excellent displays for Forest and was on the verge of the England squad but lost his place to Mark Crossley at the end of the 1989-90 season. The Sheffield-born 'keeper made a name for himself with his fine save from Gary Lineker's penalty-kick in the FA Cup Final of 1991 and has at the time of writing played in 355 first team games for Forest.

GOALSCORING

For the club:

Forest's highest goalscoring tallies were achieved in 1950-51 when the club won the Third Division (South) championship and scored 110 goals in 46 matches and in 1956-57 when the club scored 94 goals to finish as runners-up in the Second Division.

For the individual:

The following players have scored 50 or more League goals for the club:

Grenville Morris	1898-1913	199
Wally Ardron	1949-1955	123
Johnny Dent	1929-1936	119
Ian Storey-Moore	1963-1972	105
Nigel Clough	1984-1995	101
Enoch West	1905-1910	93
Tommy Wilson	1951-1960	75
Garry Birtles	1977-1980/1982-1987	70
Tommy Capel	1949-1954,	69
Ian Bowyer	1973-1980/1981-1987	68
Billy Dickinson	1928-1934,	68
Jim Barrett	1954-1959,	64
Colin Addison	1961-1966,	62
John Roberston	1970-1982/1985-1986	61
Noah Burton	1921-1931,	57
Tommy Peacock	1933-1939,	57
Peter Davenport	1981-1986	54
Syd Gibson	1921-1928	53
John Quigley	1957-1965	51
Steve Hodge	1982-1985/1988-1991	50

All dates refer to calendar years of debuts and last appearances, correct to August 1998

GOALSCORING EXPLOITS

Alex Higgins was the first Nottingham Forest player to score as many as five goals in a competitive match. He did so in the 14-0 FA Cup win over Clapton Orient in 1890-91. Higgins scored four goals on two occasions that season in the Football Alliance against Darwen and Crewe Alexandra; a hat-trick against Newton Heath in the same competition, plus another in the FA Cup against Sunderland Albion. The following season, Higgins hit four in the Alliance against Lincoln City and another League hat-trick against Grimsby Town. Between September 1890 and April 1894 he scored 89 goals in 107 matches for the club.

Nottingham Forest are the holders of two goalscoring records - their 14-0 victory over Clapton Orient in the 1890-91 FA Cup competition was the biggest away win in English first-class football and their 12-0 win over Leicester Fosse in 1909 stands as the greatest Division One victory.

Joining Forest in 1933, Tom Peacock was a superb marksman and in the months of November and December 1935, he scored four goals in a game on three occasions against Barnsley, Port Vale and Doncaster Rovers.

Signed from Rotherham United in July 1949, Wally Ardron scored 25 goals in his first season with the club and then in 1950-51, he scored 36 goals, which is still a club record.

GRAHAM, TOMMY

Tommy Graham attracted the attention of a number of League clubs with his impressive performances at wing-half for his local side, Consett Celtic. However, it was Nottingham Forest who signed this most popular player in July 1927. He made his League debut for the Reds towards the end of the following season in a goalless draw against Bristol City at Ashton Gate.

He won a regular place in the Forest line-up the following campaign as a replacement for the injured Bob Wallace but also had to cover for Percy Barratt who like Wallace had suffered a long-term injury.

With Wallace fully recovered and Jimmy Barrington now at left-back, Graham only played 24 League games in that 1929-30 season.

He eventually regained a regular place in the Forest side at centre-half at the expense of Albert Harrison and went on to become one of the best number fives in the country. In fact, he turned in so many impressive displays that Forest had to turn down a number of offers for their star player from top clubs. It came as no surprise in 1931 when he won two caps for England against France and Northern Ireland.

Though he continued to play for Forest during the war years, he played the last of his 390 League and Cup games against Plymouth Argyle in April 1939. Appointed club trainer, he was forced to give up this position in 1961 but continued his connection with the club right up to his death by working as a scout.

GRAY, BILLY

Joining Leyton Orient from Dinnington Colliery, the Durham-born winger soon attracted the attention of the bigger clubs and was snapped up by Chelsea in March 1949. He spent four years at Stamford Bridge, scoring 12 goals in his 146 League appearances and winning an England 'B' cap before signing for Burnley in June 1953 for £16,000.

He ended his first season at Turf Moor as the club's top scorer with 19 goals after scoring six times in his first seven games. He was a virtual ever-present on the Clarets' right-wing until he joined Nottingham Forest in the summer of 1957.

The City Ground club were shrewd enough to convert him into a scheming inside-forward and later to a full-back to get the best out of him. He won an FA Cup winners' medal in 1959 and was a member of Forest's first ever team to compete in Europe, although the experience was a sobering one as Valencia of Spain beat the Reds both home and away in the first round of the Inter Cities Fairs Cup. Gray played the last of his 223 League and Cup games for Forest in April 1963 just a month short of his 36th birthday before joining Millwall as player-manager seven months later.

Though the Lions were relegated to the Fourth Division, within two years he had reversed their fortunes and they were back in the Second Division.

He later managed Brentford and Notts County before returning to the City Ground as Forest's groundsman.

GRAY, FRANK

A former Parkhead ball-boy, Frank Gray went to Leeds United in the summer of 1970 after the Yorkshire club signed him in the face of stiff competition from a number of other clubs. He turned professional in November 1971 and scored on his full debut in a 4-0 home win over Crystal Palace. After winning five Scottish Under-23 caps, he won the first of 32 full caps when he played against England at St James' Park in March 1974.

In July 1979 he moved to Nottingham Forest for a then Leeds club record fee of £500,000. Under Brian Clough, Gray enjoyed the best years of his career. After making his Forest debut in a 1-0 win at Ipswich Town on the opening day of the 1979-80 season, he went on to play in 118 League and Cup games in two seasons at the City Ground. Also with Forest, in 1980 he won a European Cup winners' medal to go with the one he won with Leeds in 1975. He returned to Elland Road in May 1981 and was Scotland's left-back in the 1982 World Cup in Spain.

Gray had played in 401 first team games for Leeds when, in 1985, he was transferred by brother Eddie to Sunderland. He helped the Wearsiders win promotion from Division Three before being appointed player-assistant manager at Darlington. Later after scouting for a number of clubs, he became manager of Harrogate Town before taking charge of Al Mananmah in Bahrain. His son Andy, who also played for Leeds United, has recently joined Forest.

GRUMMITT, PETER

Signed from Bourne Town in May 1960, Peter Grummitt turned in a number of impressive displays in the Football Combination before being given his League debut against Bolton Wanderers at the City Ground on 12 November 1960. He was aged 18 and though his first touch of the ball was to pick it out of the net after Jim Iley had put through his own goal, he went on to make the number one spot his own over the next nine seasons.

Though he went on to represent the Football League and England Under-23 side, he was never to win a full cap – surely one of the best goalkeepers never to do so.

He was an ever-present in 1966-67 when Forest reached the FA Cup semi-final and were runners-up in the First Division. At Elland

Road in 1968, the unfortunate Grummitt broke his arm but when fully recovered he was unable to regain his place from Alan Hill. Surprisingly, after 352 first team appearances, the popular Grummitt was allowed to leave the City Ground and joined Sheffield Wednesday where he made 121 League appearances in four years at Hillsborough. Again injury cut short his stay in Yorkshire and he ended his career with Brighton, having played in 570 League games for his three clubs.

GUEST PLAYERS

The 'guest' system was used by all clubs during the two wars. Although at times it was abused almost beyond belief (some sides that opposed Forest had ten or eleven 'guests'!) it normally worked sensibly and effectively to the benefit of the players, clubs and supporters alike.

During the First World War, Danny Shea an inside-forward from Blackburn Rovers, Noah Burton an outside left from Derby County, Sunderland's Harry Martin and the ex-England 'keeper Sam Hardy all 'guested' for Forest and with these players in their ranks, Forest won the Victory Shield in 1919.

In the Second World war, Birmingham City and England goalkeeper Gil Merrick 'guested' for the Reds as did George Hardwick the Middlesborough, Oldham Athletic and England full-back.

H

HARDY, SAM

One of the most famous goalkeepers England have ever had, he played his early football with Newbold White Star in Derbyshire before joining Chesterfield in 1902. Even though he conceded six goals in a match against Liverpool, he impressed the Merseysiders so much that they signed him for £500 in October 1905.

In his first season at Anfield, Liverpool took the title with Hardy in superb form. In 1907 he played for England in all three home internationals. In all he represented his country on 21 occasions. In May 1912 he was surprisingly transferred to Aston Villa where he played in the 1913 and 1920 FA Cup Finals.

During the First World War he served in the Royal Navy. He guested for Forest when the Reds won the Victory Shield in 1919, beating Everton 1-0 at Goodison Park. It was August 1921 before he eventually signed for Forest and made his debut at Crystal Palace on the opening day of the season when the Reds went down 4-1. It was only a minor setback as Hardy only conceded 23 goals in his 32 League appearances to help Forest win the Second Division title.

He played in 109 League and Cup games for Forest, keeping 41 clean sheets before an injury sustained against Newcastle United on 4 October 1924 forced him to retire at the age of 41.

HAT-TRICKS

The club's first hat-trick in the Football League was scored by débutante James Collins in Forest's 7-1 win over Wolverhampton Wanderers on 2 September 1893.

Wally Ardron and Tom Peacock have both scored six hat-tricks for Forest whilst Johnny Dent, Grenville Morris and Enoch West have all scored five.

When Forest beat Leicester Fosse 12-0 on 21 April 1909, Spouncer, Hooper and West each scored a hat-trick. There have been six occasions when two Forest players have scored hat-tricks in the same match, though three of these were in wartime games. The first came in the 14-0 FA Cup win over Clapton in 1890-91 when Higgins 5 and Lindley 4 helped the Reds to their record win. The first instance in the Football League came in 1950-51 when Capel 4 and Ardron 3 scored in Forest's 9-2 home win over Gillingham. In 1986-87, Webb and Birtles each grabbed a hat-trick as the Reds beat Chelsea 6-2 at Stamford Bridge. During the First World War, Birch 4 and Tinsley 3 helped Forest defeat Chesterfield 8-1 in the Subsidiary Tournament of the Midland Section. In the second World War, Beaumont and Flewitt each scored a hat-trick as Forest beat Lincoln City 8-1 and in the last season before peacetime football resumed, Johnson and O'Donnell scored three goals apiece in the 7-2 thrashing of Newport County.

HENNESSEY, TERRY

A cultured wing-half with Birmingham City for whom he made 203 appearances, he signed for Forest in November 1965 as the eventual replacement for long-serving Jeff Whitefoot. Making his League debut for the Reds in the 2-1 home win over Blackpool, when both Forest's goals were scored by the opposition, he went on to play in 183 first team games.

Only 23 when he arrived at the City Ground, he looked much older because of his receding hairline. Showing a great maturity in his play, the Welsh-born player won 39 caps for his country, 15 of them during his stay at the City Ground.

In 1966-67 he was appointed Forest's captain and led the Reds to a FA Cup semi-final where they lost 2-1 to Spurs and to runners-up spot in the First Division.

One of the players Matt Gillies allowed to leave, he joined Derby County in February 1970 as the Rams' first £100,000 signing and in 1971-72 won a League Championship medal. After injury cut short his playing career the following season, he managed non-League Tamworth and Kimberley Town before coaching Tulsa Rougnecks in the NASL.

HIGGINS, 'SANDY'

One of the most unlucky of all international players, he scored four goals in Scotland's 8-2 win over Ireland in 1885 but was never se-lected again! Playing for a number of Scottish clubs, though notably with Kilmarnock, he came south of the border in August 1888 to join Derby County. Playing in their first game in the Football League, he was the Rams' leading scorer for two seasons before joining Forest at the end of the 1889-90 season.

In his first season at the club he scored 35 goals, including four in a 7-0 win at Crewe and all four in a 4-4 draw at Darwen. In 1891-92 he scored 34 goals and set the club record of five goals in one game, scored in the 14-0 win against Clapton in January 1891, even though he'd been declared unfit for the match!

Though he found goals harder to come by in the Football League, he was the club's top scorer in their first season with 12 goals and scored both goals against Everton as Forest drew their opening match 2-2. He retired in April 1894 after scoring 36 goals in 64 League and Cup appearances.

His son Alexander also played for Forest but was released at the end of the 1920-21 season after just 35 first team appearances.

HINDLEY, PETER

The son of Frank Hindley who played for Forest just before the Second World War, he joined the Reds as a centre-forward, signing professional forms in the summer of 1961.

He made his debut at Everton on 9 March 1963 but was switched to centre-half shortly afterwards and used in manager Andy Beattie's 'double centre-half' ploy. However, the Worksop-born player found his chances limited by the magnificent consistency of Bobby McKinlay. Moving to right-back, Hindley formed a solid partnership with John Winfield. He was an ever-present in 1966-67 when Forest were runners-up in the First Division and so outstanding was his form that he was selected for the England Under-23 team. After appearing in 416 League and Cup games for the Reds, he lost his first team place to Liam O'Kane and was allowed to join Coventry City in January 1974. After just 33 appearances for the Highfield Road club he moved to Peterborough United where he played in 112 League games before retiring.

HODGE, STEVE

Nottingham-born Steve Hodge made his League debut for the reds against Ipswich town in the last game of the 1981-82 season when Forest won the Portman Road encounter 3-1. The following season he became a first team regular, playing in either midfield or on the wing and had played in 150 first team games before in August 1985 he signed for Aston Villa for £400,000.

In his first season at Villa Park he won the first of his 24 England caps and had an outstanding World Cup in 1986. It was his performance in this tournament that led to his big money transfer to Tottenham Hotspur. His form suffered at White Hart Lane and in 1988 after only 45 League appearances for Spurs, he returned to the City Ground for £575,000.

Playing some of the best football of his career, he won his England place back and gained League Cup winners' medals. He had appeared in 274 first team games for Forest before joining Leeds United. He later went on loan to Derby County and played for Queen's Park Rangers before ending his League career with Watford.

Steve Hodge in action during his Leeds United days.

HOME MATCHES

Nottingham Forest's biggest victory is the 12-0 rout of Leicester Fosse on 21 April 1909 in a First Division fixture. Forest have also won two home matches by a 9-2 scoreline, these were Port Vale (Division Two 1935-36) and Gillingham (Division Three (South) 1950-51). Forest have scored seven goals in a home fixture on ten occasions, keeping a clean sheet on four: Preston North End (Division Two 1926-27); Fulham (Division Two 1927-28); Aldershot (Division Three (South) 1950-51) and Chelsea (Division One 1990-91).

Forest's worst home defeat is 7-1, a scoreline inflicted upon them by Birmingham City in a Division One match on 7 March 1959. The only other time Forest have conceded seven goals at home came in season 1903-04 when Aston Villa won 7-3 in a First Division encounter.

The highest scoring home match other than those mentioned above is Forest's 6-4 victory over Swansea Town on 27 September 1952.

HOME SEASONS

Nottingham Forest have gone through a complete League season with an undefeated home record on two occasions:

1977-78	Division One	Won 15	Drew 6
1978-79	Division One	Won 11	Drew 10

Forest's highest number of home wins in a League season is 18. They achieved this figure in 1997-98 when winning the First Division championship.

HONOURS

The major honours achieved by the club are:

Division One	Champions	1977-78 (pre-Premier), 1997-98 (formerly Div. 2)
	Runners-Up	1966-67, 1978-79, 1993-94 (as above)
Division Two	Champions	1906-07, 1921-22
	Runners-Up	1956-57
Division Three (South)	Champions	1950-51
Football Alliance	Champions	1891-92
Anglo Scottish Cup	Winners	1976-77
Charity Shield	Winners	1978
	Finalists	1959
European Cup	Winners	1978-79, 1979-80
FA Cup	Winners	1897-98, 1958-59
	Finalists	1990-91
League Cup	Winners	1977-78, 1978-79, 1988-89, 1989-90
	Finalists	1979-80, 1991-92
UEFA Super Cup	Winners	1979-80
	Finalists	1980-81
World Club Championship	Finalists	1980
Simod Cup	Winners	1988-89
Zenith Data Cup	Winners	1991-92

HUTCHINSON, JACK

Born at Heanor, Derbyshire, Jack Hutchinson joined Forest as a junior during the Second World War. Having played all his early football at inside-forward, he made his Forest League debut as a full-back against Millwall on 9 November 1946.

Jack Hutchinson was a top-class defender whose positional sense and distribution were outstanding. Yet despite being at the City Ground for 12 years he only played in 254 League and Cup games. This was because his first team opportunities with Forest were limited by Bill Whare and Geoff Thomas, the club being very fortunate to have three such full-backs during the same period.

It was Hutchinson who missed out on the 1959 FA Cup Final victory over Luton Town after which he decided to retire.

I

ILEY, JIM

When Jim Iley signed for Sheffield United, he combined playing part-time with a job at Frickley Colliery before turning professional. In four years at Bramhall Lane, Iley made over 100 appearances for the Yorkshire club and gained his first senior representative honours when he played for the Football League against the Irish League.

In April 1956 he joined Tottenham Hotspur and though he took time to settle, he was soon capped by England at Under-23 level. After Dave Mackay arrived at White Hart Lane, Iley found himself surplus to requirements and moved to Nottingham Forest for £16,000.

After scoring on his debut in a 2-1 defeat by Manchester City on the opening day of the 1959-60 season, Iley went on to appear in 103 League and Cup games for Forest in a little over three years at the City Ground before joining Newcastle United. It was at St James' Park that Iley enjoyed the best period of his career and he was a solid regular for six years. In January 1969 he became player-manager of Peterborough United before going on to manage Barnsley, Blackburn Rovers, Bury and Exeter City.

IMLACH, STEWART

Introduced into English football by Bury in May 1952, he scored 14 goals in 71 League games for the Shakers before joining Derby County two years later. But within twelve months, the Rams had been relegated to the Third Division (North) and he joined Forest.

He made his League debut against Liverpool in the opening game of the 1955-56 season and went on to become a great favourite with the crowd. The Scottish-born winger possessed good ball control and a fierce shot with either foot. He won four Scottish caps and appeared in the 1958 World Cup Finals in Sweden as well as gaining an FA Cup winners' medal when Forest beat Luton Town in 1959.

After scoring 48 goals in 204 League and Cup games he left for Luton Town in June 1960 but after just eight League appearances for the Hatters, he moved on to Coventry City before ending his League career with Crystal Palace. Moving into non-League football with Dover and Chelmsford City, he later held coaching positions with Notts County, Everton, Blackpool and Bury.

INJURIES

The risk of serious injury is an ever-present threat in the game of football and all professional players expect to miss games through injury at some point in their careers.

The most notable Forest casualty was Roy Dwight who, after having scored the opening goal in the 1959 FA Cup Final win over Luton Town, was stretchered off the field with a broken leg - the infamous Wembley 'hoodoo' had struck again.

INTER CITIES FAIRS CUP

Nottingham Forest entered Europe for the first time in competition in 1961-62, playing in the Inter Cities Fairs Cup.

Their opponents were Spanish giants Valencia who thrashed the Reds 7-1 over two legs, winning the second leg at the City Ground 5-1. The scorer of Forest's consolation goal, their first in Europe was Bill Cobb.

Forest's second appearance in the Inter Cities Fairs Cup was in 1967-68 but after beating Eintracht Frankfurt 5-0 over two legs, the Reds were knocked out of the competition on aslight technicality. After winning the home leg against FC Zurich 2-1 they travelled to Switzerland to play the away leg, which Forest lost 1-0. However, while the Swiss team left the field in jubilation at the end of the game, ten red shirts stood in the middle of the pitch waiting for extra-time that never came. As Terry Hennessey later confessed, 'We didn't know the rules'.

INTERNATIONAL PLAYERS

Nottingham Forest's most capped player (i.e. caps gained while players were registered with the club) is Stuart Pearce with 76 caps. The following is a complete list of players who have gained full international honours while at the City Ground.

England

V.A. Anderson	11
G. Birtles	3
F.E. Burton	1
J. Calvey	1
N.H. Clough	14
S. Collymore	2
C.T. Cooper	2
T. Danks	1
P. Davenport	1
F. Forman	9
F.R. Forman	3
T.J. Francis	10
A.C. Goodyer	1
T. Graham	2
A.T. Hinton	2
S.B. Hodge	9
J. Iremonger	2
H. Jones	1
J.E. Leighton	1
J.H. Linacre	2
T. Lindley	4
L.V. Lloyd	1
E. Luntley	2
S. Pearce	76
C.H. Richards	1
J. Sands	1
P.L. Shilton	19
A. Smith	3
W.A. Spouncer	1
S.B. Stone	9
I. Storey-Moore	1
D.S. Walker	47
N.J. Webb	18
S.W. Widdowson	1
F. Wignall	2
A.S. Woodcock	6

Scotland

K. Burns	12
P.B. Cormack	5
A. Gemmill	11
S. Gemmill	13
F.T. Gray	7
J.J.S. Imlach	4
J.N. Robertson	26

Wales

A.W. Green	2
W.T. Hennessey	15
E. Hughes	9
A.T. Jones	1
C. Jones	4
A.G. Morris	16
R.R. Rees	16

Northern Ireland

K. Black	14
D.A. Campbell	7
J. Chambers	3
F. Coyle	1
J.G. Fleming	9
J. Hanna	2
T. Jackson	19
D.K. Martin	4
F.G. Morgan	6
P. Nelis	1
W.J. O'Kane	20
M.H.M. O'Neill	36

Republic of Ireland

J. Dennehy	7
R. Keane	16
N. Kelly	1

Forest's first player to be capped was A.C. Goodyer who played for England v Scotland on 5 April 1879.

Ronnie Rees, who won 16 caps for Wales whilst with Forest.

IREMONGER, JIM

Jim Iremonger played for local clubs Wilford FC and Jardine's FC before joining Forest in 1896. Making his debut at left-back in a 1-0 defeat at Stoke, he had to wait until 1897-98 before winning a regular place in the Forest side but even then he did not feature in the Reds' FA Cup Final side of that season.

After Archie Ritchie and Adam Scott had retired, Jim Iremonger came into his own, eventually winning caps for England in 1901 against Scotland and a year later against Ireland.

The brother of the famous Notts County goalkeeper Albert Iremonger, he too was a good 'keeper and in 1906-07 he reverted to this position. He was between the sticks on 21 April 1909 when Forest beat Leicester Fosse 12-0 – probably the quietest afternoon of his career.

After playing in 300 League and Cup games for Forest, he retired and later became coach at Notts County.

Despite spending 15 seasons with Forest, he will always be best remembered as a cricketer. He made his debut for Nottinghamshire in 1897 and was a fine all-rounder, scoring 16,110 runs and taking 696 wickets. He later became coach at Trent Bridge from 1921 to 1938.

JACKDAW

In the years immediately following the Second World War on first team match days at the City Ground, a jackdaw boarded a Nottingham Corporation bus at Council House Square and alighted at Trent Bridge from whence it flew to the City Ground to watch Nottingham Forest.

JONES, HARRY

Derbyshire-born Harry Jones played for both Blackwell Wesley Guild and Blackwell Colliery before signing for Nottingham Forest in the close season of 1911. He made his debut in the 1912-13 season, starring in the 3-2 win over Glossop at the City Ground.

During the First World War he sustained a broken leg which threatened his future footballing career but happily he recovered to play a leading role in the Victory Shield match in 1919.

Appointed club captain after the war, he formed an outstanding full-back pairing with his closest friend Harry Bulling and won recognition for his performances with an England cap against France in 1923. He was then 31, but had in the past represented the Football League.

During the 1914-15 season he was asked to play up front and responded with a hat-trick in the 6-1 FA Cup qualifying round win over Shrewsbury Town.

After playing in 240 first team games for Forest, he retired through injury but came back a few months later to play for Sutton Town.

K

KEANE, ROY

Signed from Cobh Ramblers in the Republic of Ireland during the 1990 close season, Brian Clough plunged him straight into first team action against Liverpool the then League Champions. In a season where it was expected that he would have difficulties getting into the reserve side, he made 35 League appearances, scoring eight goals.

On 22 May 1991 he won his first full cap when playing for the Republic of Ireland against Chile in Dublin. He had another excellent season in 1991-92 helping Forest to two finals, defeating Southampton 3-2 in the Zenith Data Systems Cup Final but losing 1-0 to Manchester United in the League Cup Final.

A midfield player with plenty of stamina, he had scored 33 goals in 154 games for Forest before joining Manchester United for a fee of £3.75 million in July 1993.

At Old Trafford, Keane has taken his total of appearances for the Republic of Ireland to 38 and has won three championship medals as United won four titles in five years. Injured after only playing in nine League games in 1997-98, Keane is now back to full fitness.

Roy Keane, now with Manchester United.

L

LANGFORD, LEN

One of the game's great characters, he joined the Coldstream Guards at the age of 15 and served with them throughout the First World War. After the hostilities ended, he signed for Rossington Colliery FC and it was from there that he joined Forest in 1925.

Making his debut against Sheffield United in a 3-2 home defeat on 14 February 1925, he soon displaced Arthur Bennett as the Reds' first-choice goalkeeper and after playing in 40 games the following season was an ever-present in 1926-27.

After playing in 144 League and Cup games for Forest, he signed for Manchester City in 1930 and gained a FA Cup runners-up medal in 1933. After 125 first team appearances at Maine Road he moved across the city to play 15 League games for Manchester United.

Len Langford was also something of an all-round sportsman, being middleweight boxing champion of the Household Brigade in 1920 and 1921. A keen cricketer, he was also keen on athletics, winning trophies for the high-jump.

LARGEST CROWD

It was on 28 October 1967 that the City Ground housed its largest crowd. The occasion was a First Division match against Manchester United. The crowd was a staggering 49,946 who witnessed Forest winning 3-1 with two goals from Joe Baker and one from Frank Wignall.

LAST GASP GOALS

When Forest reached the FA Cup Final for the first time in their history in 1898 they had two last-minute goals from Tom McInnes and Chas Richards that helped them defeat Southampton 2-0 in the semi-final replay at Crystal Palace after the clubs had drawn 1-1 at Bramall Lane.

LATE FINISHES

Nottingham Forest's latest finish to a Football League season was 14 June in the 1946-47 season, when a Tommy Johnston hat-trick helped them beat Bradford 4-0 at the City Ground.

During the Second World War many curious things occurred and in 1939-40, Forest lost their last game on 8 June 4-3 at Grimsby. The following season, Forest played their final game on 6 June, going down 2-0 at home to Leicester City. The game prior to this on 24 May saw Forest beat Walsall at Fellowes Park 7-6!

LEADING GOALSCORERS

Nottingham Forest have provided the Football League's leading divisional goalscorer on three occasions.

In 1907-08 Enoch West led the Division One charts with 27 goals whilst in 1973-74, Duncan McKenzie topped the Division Two table with 26 goals. In 1997-98, Pierre van Hooijdonk headed the Division One charts with 29 goals, a total equalled by Sunderland's Kevin Phillips.

LEEDS CITY

Founder members of the Second Division in 1892, they were never promoted during their ten seasons. Forest played them on ten occasions, the first being on 22 September 1906 when goals from Morris (2) and Shearman gave the Reds a 3-0 win. They completed the 'double' later in the season, winning 4-1 in Yorkshire. Both clubs won their home matches in 1911-12 the next season they met before Leeds did the 'double' the following season. In 1913-14 Forest lost 8-0 at Leeds but won the return 2-1 thanks to goals from Derrick and Harris. The clubs last met in 1914-15, Forest winning 3-1 at the City Ground but going down 4-0 on 10 April 1915, the last time the clubs played each other.

Leeds City were expelled from the League in 1919 after making illegal payments during wartime matches.

LEICESTER FOSSE

When Forest beat Leicester Fosse 12-0 in a First Division match on 21 April 1909, they were at the time in danger of relegation and after such a surprise result, an inquiry was held. In the official findings, it was mentioned that the Fosse players had attended the wedding celebrations of a colleague on the previous day!

LINACRE, HAROLD

Born in the Derbyshire village of Aston-on-Trent in 1881, Harry Linacre was the nephew of Frank and Fred Forman. He played for Loughborough Grammar School, Aston-on-Trent and Draycott Mills and made two League appearances for Derby County before in August 1899, he signed for Nottingham Forest on the recommendation of Frank Forman.

Making his League debut in a 2-2 draw at home to Bury on 4 November 1899, he went on to prove an outstanding replacement for Dennis Allsop, Forest's veteran goalkeeper. In his first full season he was an ever-present and only conceded 36 goals in his 34 appearances as Forest finished fourth in the First Division.

A firm favourite with the Forest fans, he won two England caps, both in 1905 against Scotland and Wales.

He won a Second Division championship medal in 1907 and also represented the Football League. He played his last game for Forest against the same opposition as he'd faced on his debut but unfortunately this time Bury won 2-0. He left the club in the close season of 1909 and, not surprisingly, two seasons later Forest were relegated.

LINDLEY, TINSLEY

One of the most famous amateur players of his generation, he made his England debut in 1886, scoring in a 6-1 win over Ireland in Belfast.

Born in Nottingham, he was a Cambridge Blue and a centre-forward with the great Corinthians side. He also played for Casuals, Crusaders and Notts County as well as Forest, though it is unclear as to which club he was attached and at what time.

Something of a character, he always refused to wear football boots, claiming they reduced his speed, preferring to wear ordinary walking shoes instead. He scored four times when Forest beat Clapton 14-0 on 17 January 1891 and 15 FA Cup goals in 25 appearances in the competition.

In 1899 he was called to the bar and lectured on law at Nottingham University before becoming a county court judge. In 1918 he was awarded the OBE for his work as chief officer of Nottingham's Special Constabulary.

LLOYD, LARRY

After progressing through the junior teams at Eastville, he made the first of 43 League appearances for Bristol Rovers before being signed by Bill Shankly for £50,000.

A vital member of the Liverpool squad, he helped the Merseyside club to the League Championship, the UEFA Cup and into a FA Cup Final as well as winning three England caps. Injuries and a loss of form after 150 League games for Liverpool resulted in his £225,000 transfer to Coventry City just before the start of the 1974-75 season.

Whilst at Highfield Road he came to Forest on loan before signing for £60,000 in October 1976. Making his Forest debut at Hull City that month, he began to form a superb partnership at the heart of the Forest defence with Kenny Burns. He won a League Championship medal in 1977-78, though he missed over three months through injury.

Larry Lloyd

He had an outstanding season in 1979-80 when he was ever-present and voted Forest's Player of the Year. He also won his fourth cap for England but it was perhaps a performance he would rather forget as Wales won 4-1 at the Racecourse Ground.

Lloyd joined Wigan Athletic in 1981, becoming manager at Springfield Park and guiding the Latics to promotion. Appointed manager of Notts County in 1983, he led them to the top of the First Division before relegation and his dismissal soon followed.

LONGEST LEAGUE RUNS

Undefeated Matches	42	(26 November 1977- 25 November 1978)
Undefeated Home Matches	51	(27 April 1977 - 17 November 1979)
Without Home Win	10	(20 November 1909 - 9 April 1910)
League Wins	7	(24 December 1892 - 25 February 1893), (29 August 1921 - 1 October 1921)
League Defeats	14	(8 February 1913 - 18 November 1913)
Without a Win	16	(15 March 1913 - 8 October 1913)
Undefeated Away Matches	21	(3 December 1977 - 9 December 1978)
Without an Away Win	37	(25 January 1913 - 23 January 1915)
Home Wins	12	(23 February 1980 - 20 September 1980)
Away Wins	5	(23 March 1906 - 20 April 1906), (31 December 1988 - 25 March 1989), (21 November 1993 - 16 January 1994)

LONG SERVICE

One of the club's most illustrious personalities is Billy Walker who joined Forest as manager in March 1939. He led the club to promotion on two occasions and to victory in the 1959 FA Cup Final. Feeling somewhat jaded, he resigned in the summer of 1960 but was delighted to be offered a position on the club's committee. However, in 1963 he suffered a stroke and passed away on 28 November 1964.

Brian Clough joined Forest as manager in January 1975. Until his arrival, the Reds had only won two major trophies (the FA Cup twice) in the history. He led them to seven more - the Football League title, two European Cups and four League Cups. He was also 'Manager of the Year' in 1977-78. He resigned at the end of the 1992-93 season after 18 years at the City Ground.

A number of players have also served the club well. Bobby McKinlay joined the club in October 1949, made his debut in 1951 and made his final appearance in November 1969, a total of 20 years at the City Ground. Jack Armstrong made his Leagued debut for the Reds in 1905 and went on to give 17 years splendid service to the club in every position except goalkeeper and full-back. Frank Forman was released by Derby County in 1894 and joined his brother Fred at Nottingham Forest. Making his debut on 16 March 1895, he served the club as a player for 11 years before on his retirement, joining the committee. Elected a life member of the club, he died in 1961, aged 86.

Making his League debut on 22 February 1928, Tommy Graham went on to make 390 League and Cup appearances for the Reds and continued playing throughout the war. In 1944 he was appointed club trainer but was forced to give up the position due to ill health in 1961. However, the popular Graham maintained his connection with the club, working as a scout and advising the youth team.

Jimmy Barrington joined Forest from Wigan Borough in 1929. After six seasons and 228 appearances he was given a free transfer. There was such an outcry from Forest supporters that he was immediately reinstated. After playing his last game on Christmas Day 1936, he continued to work for the club as a scout until the late 1950s.

Other players who have served the club well include: Jim Iremonger (1896-1909); Ian Bowyer (1973-1987); Jack Burkitt (1948-1961); Sammy Chapman (1964-1977); Grenville Morris (1898-1913) and Geoff Thomas (1946-1960).

LOWEST

The lowest number of goals scored by Nottingham Forest in a single Football League season is 29 in 1924-25 when the club finished bottom of the First Division and were relegated.

The lowest points record in the Football League occurred in 1913-14 when Forest gained just 23 points to finish twentieth in the Second Division.

LYONS, BARRY

After an unsuccessful trial at the City Ground whilst playing with Shirebrook Miners' Welfare, the popular winger joined Rotherham United in 1962. Forest eventually signed him for £45,000 in November 1966 after he had scored 24 goals in 125 League games for the Millmoor club.

Forming a devastating wing combination with Ian Storey-Moore, Lyons once seemed on the verge of an England Under-23 cap. Though his performances lacked a little in consistency, there can be no doubting his commitment. After playing in 239 first team games for the

Barry Lyons

Reds, he lost his place and in September 1973 following Forest's relegation to the Second Division, he was transferred to York City.

He played an important role in York's promotion to the Second Division before joining Darlington at the end of the 1975-76 season. After ending his playing days at the Feethams, he returned to Bootham Crescent as coach. From May 1980 to December 1981 he was York manager but reverted to youth team coach before leaving the club for a second time in July 1982.

M

MACKAY, DAVE

One of the great players of his era, Dave Mackay won just about every honour in the game during his long and distinguished career.

With Hearts, Mackay won two Scottish League Cup winners' medals, a Scottish Cup winners' medal and ended his time at Tynecastle with a League Championship medal in 1958. Bill Nicholson signed him for Spurs in March 1959 for £30,000. He became one of Tottenham's greatest-ever players, helping the club to the League and FA Cup double in 1961 and retaining the Cup the following year. He won a third FA Cup winners' medal in 1967 when he captained the side to victory over Chelsea. He broke his leg twice whilst at White Hart Lane but recovered to full fitness on both occasions. Perhaps one of the games greatest mysteries is why he only won 22 caps for Scotland.

In July 1968 Brian Clough signed Mackay for Derby County for just £5,000. In three seasons at the Baseball Ground he inspired the Rams to the Second Division championship and was elected joint Footballer of the Year in 1969.

In 1971 he began his management career at Swindon Town but in November 1972 he replaced Matt Gillies as Forest manager. A popular figure at the City Ground, he was a character who commanded great respect. Forest ended his first season in charge in mid-table. In October 1973 just as things seemed to be improving, he left the City Ground to replace Brian Clough at Derby. Stepping into a hornet's nest at the Baseball Ground, he rose to the challenge and took the side to the League Championship in 1974-75 and a FA Cup semi-final the following year.

Resigning in November 1976, he later managed Walsall, Doncaster Rovers and Birmingham City.

MACPHERSON, JOHN

Born at Motherwell in February 1867, John MacPherson began his footballing career with non-League Cambuslang before joining Heart of Midlothian. Forming a famous half-back line with Hill and Begbie, he helped Hearts win the Scottish FA Cup in 1891, the same season in which he won his only Scottish cap as they lost 2-1 to England.

In May 1981 he signed for Forest and was an ever-present as the Reds reached the semi-final of the FA Cup. He rejoined the Tynecastle club at the end of that season but was back at the City Ground in September 1892 to make his League debut at Aston Villa the following month.

Appointed club captain two seasons later, he was an extremely popular player and led the Reds to their first FA Cup success in 1898 when Forest beat Derby County 3-1.

He left Forest in 1901 after playing in 259 first team games to sign for his home-town club, before later emigrating to Canada.

MALTBY, GEORGE

'Ginger' Maltby as he was known, was spotted playing for Notts Rangers and was signed by Forest in 1906. Aged 19, he walked straight into the Forest first team, making his debut in the 3-0 home win over Leeds City on 22 September of that year.

He formed an effective full-back partnership with Walter Dudley who took the young defender under his wing and helped him mature as a footballer.

Strong in the tackle and quick to recover, 'Ginger' Maltby played in 230 first team games for Forest before losing his place to Tom Gibson in 1913, after which he moved on.

MANAGERS

This is the complete list of Forest's full-time managers with the inclusive dates in which they held office:

Harry Radford	1889-1897
Harry Haslam	1897-1909
Fred Earp	1909-1912
Bob Masters	1912-1925
John Baynes	1925-1929
Stan Hardy	1930-1931
Noel Watson	1931-1936
Harold Wightman	1936-1939
Billy Walker	1939-1960
Andy Beattie	1960-1963
Johnny Carey	1963-1968
Matt Gillies	1969-1972
Dave Mackay	1972
Allan Brown	1973-1975
Brian Clough	1975-1993
Frank Clark	1993-1996
Stuart Pearce	1996-1997
Dave Bassett	1997-

MARATHON MATCHES

Nottingham Forest have been involved in two cup ties that have gone into four matches. The first was in season 1922-23 when the Reds drew Sheffield United in the third round of the FA Cup. The first match at the City Ground was goalless as was the replay at Bramall Lane. The second replay at Meadow Lane, Nottingham ended all-square at 1-1 with John Green netting for Forest. The third replay was played at Hillsborough where United won by the only goal of the game.

The second occasion when Forest played four games to determine the result of a cup match was in 1974-75 when they drew Fulham in the fourth round of the FA Cup. The first match at Craven Cottage was goalless and though Neil Martin put Forest ahead in the replay at the City Ground, the Londoners equalised to take the tie to a third match. John Robertson was the Forest scorer in another 1-1 draw and so the teams returned to the City Ground for the fourth meeting. Sammy Chapman scored for the Reds but it wasn't enough to earn them a place in the next round, Fulham winning 2-1.

MARKSMEN

Six players have hit a century of goals for Nottingham Forest (including Football League, FA Cup, League Cup and European Cup). The club's top marksman is Grenville Morris. The Century Club consists of:

1.	Grenville Morris	217
2.	Nigel Clough	131
3.	Wally Ardron	124
4.	Johnny Dent	122
5.	Ian Storey-Moore	118
6.	Enoch West	100

MARTIN, DAVE

Dave 'Boy' Martin served with the Royal Ulster Rifles before beginning his footballing career with Belfast Celtic. After winning his first cap for his country in 1933, he began to attract the attention of a number of English League clubs and a year later signed for Wolverhampton Wanderers. The Belfast-born forward had a temperamental side to his character and was dismissed a number of times in his stay at Molineux. Despite this, Harry Wightman, Forest's manager signed Martin in the summer of 1936 for what was then the club's record fee.

Wightman's gamble certainly paid dividends as Martin scored 29 goals in 37 League games including ten goals in eight consecutive appearances to beat Enoch West's goalscoring record that had stood since 1907-08.

The following season the goals were not as forthcoming, though the two he scored in the final game of the season at Barnsley to save the Reds from relegation took his total to 12 in the League.

After scoring 46 goals in 84 League and Cup appearances, he joined Notts County where he ended the 1938-39 season as top scorer. He later returned to Ireland to play for Glentoran.

MARTIN, HARRY

An outstanding outside-left for Sunderland with whom he won an England cap and played in a FA Cup Final. The Selston-born player 'guested' for Forest during the First World War and was a member of the side that won the Victory Shield in 1919. He returned to Roker Park after the hostilities but in May 1922 he joined Forest on a permanent basis.

He made his debut for the Reds in the opening game of the 1922-23 season, Forest beating his former club Sunderland 1-0 in front of a 25,000 crowd. The club's regular penalty-taker during his time at the City Ground, he scored 13 goals in 114 League and Cup appearances before joining Rochdale at the end of the 1924-25 season. He became their trainer in 1929 before managing Mansfield Town from 1933 to 1935. In 1936 he joined Swindon Town as trainer and remained on the staff of the County Ground club until the early 1950s.

McCALL, BOB

Signed from his home-town club Worksop Town in 1935, Bob McCall was one of the few Forest players to appear for the club before, during and after the Second World War. Joining the club as a forward, he later settled into the half-back line, scoring his first goal in Forest colours in the 3-0 win over Millwall in March 1939.

When football resumed after the hostilities, McCall was awarded the captaincy and became the Reds' regular left-back, going on to play in 172 first team games.

Having lost his first team place to Jack Hutchinson during the 1949-50 season, he did not appear in any of Forest's games during their Third Division (South) championship winning season. He was then appointed groundsman at the City Ground and coached Forest's 'A' team, occasionally playing the odd game at centre-forward. When the club suffered an injury crisis in 1951-52, he did play in one final League game as Forest drew 1-1 at Blackpool on 22 September 1951. He later managed Worksop Town in the Midland League.

McGOVERN, JOHN

Montrose-born John McGovern served his apprenticeship at Hartle-pool United where he first came to the notice of a young manager by the name of Brian Clough. In September 1968 he followed Clough to Derby County for £7,500. He helped the Rams to win promotion from the Second Division and won a League Championship medal with the Baseball Ground club in 1972.

In 1974 he linked up with Clough again, this time at Elland Road but the popular Scot fell out of favour at Leeds when Brian Clough sensationally left the Yorkshire club.

McGovern's career was rescued in February 1975 when he signed for Nottingham Forest, thus teaming up with Clough for a fourth time. Adding vital experience to a young Forest side, he won another League Championship medal in 1977-78 and captained the Forest sides that won the European Cup in successive seasons.

Often jeered by the crowd, who failed to appreciate his vision and graft in midfield, he played the last of his 335 League and Cup games on the final day of the 1981-82 season before joining Bolton Wanderers as manager. Things did not work out for him at Burnden Park and in January 1985 he was dismissed. He later worked with non-League side Horwich RMI before teaming up with Archie Gemmill at Rotherham United.

McINNES, TOM

Born in Dumbartonshire, Tom McInnes started his football career with Clydebank School before playing for Dalmuir Thistle and New-castle East End. Later he played for Clyde from which club he signed for Nottingham Forest in 1892.

One of the best wingers of his day, he was the only ever-present in Forest's first season in the Football League, scoring 10 goals in his 30 games. Unlucky not to win international honours, he played in a Home Scots v Anglo Scots trial match in 1897 and though he impressed, it was his opposite number who was selected for the next international.

He played for Forest in the 1898 FA Cup Final and though he was moved to the right-wing to accommodate Alf Spouncer, it was a move he didn't appreciate and his efficiency was reduced. He played the last of his 185 first team games for Forest only months after that FA Cup Final appearance before returning to Scotland.

McKENZIE, DUNCAN

After joining Forest from school, he signed as a full-time professional in 1968. His League debut came at Sunderland on 20 September 1969, the only match he played that season. Back in the reserves he began to form a deadly partnership with Graham Collier but when he was given another chance at first team level he could not reproduce his top form. He had already had a loan spell at Mansfield Town in 1969-70 when he returned to Field Mill in 1972-73 for a second spell. Seven goals in his first six games for the Stags persuaded the Forest management to give him another chance.

The Grimsby-born forward responded magnificently to top the Second Division scoring charts in 1973-74 and end the season with 28 League and Cup goals in his 49 appearances. Also that season he was on the England substitutes bench for the Home International Championships but was not called upon to play.

After scoring 46 goals in 124 League and Cup games he was allowed to join Brian Clough at Leeds United for £240,000 before going on to play for Belgian club Anderlecht, Everton, Chelsea and Blackburn Rovers. The Ewood Park club traded him to NASL team Tulsa Rougnecks in exchange for Viv Busby. He ended his playing days with Chicago Sting and a spell in Hong Kong.

McKINLAY, BILLY

Glasgow-born Billy McKinlay joined Forest from Lochgelly in 1926 and after impressing in the reserves, made his debut at Molineux on 27 December 1927. Replacing Jackie Belton, the tough-tackling Scot won over the Forest fans with his work-rate and commitment. Serving Forest for ten years, he was always ready to join the forwards in any attacking move.

An ever-present in seasons 1932-33 and 1933-34, he made the last of his 356 League and Cup appearances for the club on Good Friday 1937 at Swansea. After retiring he returned to his native Glasgow where he combined working outside football with scouting for Forest. It was Billy McKinlay who was instrumental in sending his nephew Bobby McKinlay to the club.

McKINLAY, BOBBY

The McKinlay family in Lochgelly, Fife, was steeped in football tradition. Bobby's father, Rab, was a semi-professional centre-half with Cowdenbeath. Bobby was playing for Fife junior side, Bowhill Rovers as a right-winger and it was in that position that he had a week's trial in Nottingham.

He returned home to his job in a local garage, wondering whether he would get a chance of a football career in England. Seven days later came the good news that he was to be signed as soon as he was 17. The bad news was that he had lost his place on the wing with Rovers but he was offered the centre-half spot and revelled in his new position.

Bobby McKinlay made his Football League debut as an 18-year-old in Forest's Division Two match against Coventry City at Highfield Road on 27 October 1951 when he replaced the veteran Horace Gager.

He soon impressed at centre-half and was often nominated for international selection but never gained a Scottish cap. He did line up with an International XI against a Sheffield XI for a Jimmy Hagan testimonial match at Bramall Lane.

Forest's first game in Division One after winning promotion in 1957 was at the City Ground against Preston North End and McKinlay found himself facing at centre-forward, the great and versatile Tom Finney. A crowd of 33,048 saw the Reds win 2-1. The headlines dubbed McKinlay 'Tom Finney's Shadow'.

On 22 April 1959 he missed the game against Leeds United at the City Ground but the next time he was missing in the League was on 23 October 1965, a tremendous run of 265 consecutive games. During this period he had been appointed club captain, a position he relinquished after four years to Terry Hennessey.

McKinlay's 500th game for the club came in 1965, Forest's centenary year and he was awarded a testimonial match against Glasgow Celtic. The match which Forest won 2-0 attracted a crowd of 18,303 to the City Ground on Monday night 5 April 1965 and produced receipts of nearly £4,000. The actual 500th match was against Arsenal at the City Ground. Forest laid on VIP treatment including the presentation of a cocktail cabinet to mark the occasion. Forest won 3-0 with Bobby blotting out Joe Baker, soon to be a City Ground favourite.

He played his last game for Forest on 15 November 1969 at the age of 37, appearing in 614 League games - a club record that is unlikely ever to be beaten. Also that year he was awarded the Football League Long Service Medal.

When he retired from playing, he became a coach on the Forest staff under managers Matt Gillies and Johnny Carey but he was sacked when Dave Mackay took over.

Later working as a prison officer at Lowdham Grange Detention Centre near Nottingham, it remains a mystery why this fine player, who was never sent off and booked only twice was never allowed to represent his country.

MERCANTILE CREDIT CENTENARY TROPHY

The Mercantile Credit Centenary Festival took place at Wembley over the weekend of 16-17 April 1988. Qualification for the tournament was based on the number of League points won in the first 15 League games after 1 November 1987. Eight clubs came from the First Division, four from the Second Division and two each from Division's Three and Four.

Forest's 15 games after 1 November brought them six wins, five draws and four defeats. The Reds went on to win the competition, beating Sheffield Wednesday 3-2 on penalties in the final.

MIDLAND COMBINATION

Nottingham Forest's reserve side played in the Midland Combination from 1924-25 to 1926-27, with a highest position of ninth in 1925-26. They also entered the Midland Combination Cup in their last two seasons, finishing third and fourth respectively.

MIDLAND LEAGUE

Nottingham Forest have had three spells in the Midland League (1920-24; 1927-32; and 1936-58). On 25 March 1950, Scarborough reserves beat Forest reserves 2-0 at the City Ground in a Midland League game. Forest then completed 71 unbeaten home games, winning 62 and drawing nine, scoring 237 goals and conceding 47 before losing 3-2 to York City reserves, the bottom club, three and a half years later! During that run, the club won the League title in five consecutive seasons!

MILLS, GARY

The son of former Northampton player Roley Mills, he was just 16 years 302 days old when he made his League debut for Nottingham Forest in a 2-1 home win over Arsenal on 9 September 1978. Though he only made a handful of appearances over the next two seasons, at 18 he was then the youngest to appear in a European Cup Final when he played in Forest's 1-0 win over Hamburg SV in May 1980. The winner of two England Under-21 caps, he was able to play at right-back or in midfield. Mills, who had a loan spell at Derby County, played in 172 games for Forest before moving to rivals Notts County in the summer of 1987.

His performances for the Meadow Lane Club led to him joining Leicester City. He helped the Filbert Street club to promotion to the Premier League via the play-offs in 1993-94, appearing in 23 games though injury kept him out of the play-offs themselves.

In September 1994, after scoring 17 goals in 232 games for the Filberts, he returned to Notts County for £50, 000 and took his total of first team appearances to 159 before being released in the summer of 1996.

Gary Mills

MORGAN, GERRY

Starting his football career in the Irish League with Cliftonville, he moved on to Linfield where he won his first cap for his country against England at the Hawthorns in October 1922.

Signed by Forest the following month as a replacement for Jack Armstrong, Forest's veteran left-half, he made his debut in a 1-0 win over Burnley at the City Ground. In January 1923, Fred Parker the club's regular centre-half was injured and the popular Irishman moved to pivot. It was something of an inspirational move because Morgan became one of the country's top centre-halves with his heading ability being outstanding.

Striking up a fine understanding in the middle of Forest's defence with Bob Wallace and Jack Belton, Gerry Morgan went on to appear in six further international for Ireland before playing the last of his 219 League and Cup games for the club.

After leaving the City Ground, he signed for Luton Town in 1929.

MORLEY, BILL

Arriving at the City Ground during the Second World War, Nottingham-born Bill Morley worked his way through the club's junior teams before making his League debut in a 2-2 draw at West Ham United on 30 November 1946.

During the early part of his Forest career, he was regarded as a front-line player, being able to play in any forward position but after winning a regular place in the Forest line-up towards the end of the 1949-50 season, he became more of an attacking wing-half.

An important member of Forest's championship-winning side of 1950-51, he lost his place for a couple of seasons before making a marvellous comeback and appearing in all the club's games in their promotion-winning campaign of 1956-57.

Two seasons later he lost his place to Jeff Whitefoot and retired after playing the last of his 301 League and Cup games for the Reds at West Bromwich Albion on 25 April 1959.

MORRIS, GRENVILLE

'The Prince of Inside-Forwards', Welsh-born Grenville Morris began his footballing career at St Oswald's College in Ellesmere, later moving on to Builith Town and then Aberystwyth. At the age of 18 he won his first cap for his country, scoring one of the goals in a 6-1 win over Ireland at Wrexham.

With a promise of employment as a draughtsman at the local railway works, Morris signed for Swindon Town in 1897. The County Ground club considered the Welshman too light for the role of centre-forward and converted him into an inside-right. However, within a year, Forest had secured his services for £200 and on 3 December 1898 he made his debut at Bury.

He became a regular goalscorer in his time with Forest, topping the club's scoring charts in seven of his 15 seasons with the Reds. He also scored five hat-tricks for Forest – West Bromwich Albion (Away 6-1 on 20 October 1900); Bury (Home 5-1 on 10 September 1904); Manchester City (Home 3-1 on 11 April 1908); Manchester United (Away 6-2 on 27 November 1909) and Sheffield Wednesday (Away 3-4 on 11 December 1909).

He made a further 16 appearances for Wales whilst with Forest. Playing the last of his 460 League and Cup games for the Reds on 26 April 1913, scoring 217 goal, his tally of 199 League goals remains a record for Forest.

Morris was a very fit man, working in his own coal merchant's business. He was also a talented tennis player and was only forbidden from playing at Wimbledon because of his professional status.

MOST GOALS IN A SEASON

Nottingham Forest scored 110 goals in 46 Division Three (South) matches during the 1950-51 season. They failed to score in four home games and two away. 57 goals were scored at home and 53 away.

At the City Ground, Gillingham were beaten 9-2 and Aldershot 7-0 whilst away from home, Forest won 6-1 at Crystal Palace and 5-0 at Exeter City. In ten games, four or more goals were scored. The top scorer was Wally Ardron with 36 goals (including three hat-tricks) while Tommy Capel scored 23 goals. Forest secured 70 points and won the championship.

MOST MATCHES

Nottingham Forest played their most number of matches, 65, in

1979-80. This comprised 42 League games, two FA Cup games, 10 Football League Cup games, nine European Cup games when they won the Cup and two European Super Cup games when they beat Barcelona over two legs.

In the space of four weeks in the month of April 1963, Forest played the following ten matches:

Date	Opponents	Competition	Venue	Score
3 April	Southampton	FA Cup Rd 6 R	Away	3-3
6 April	Arsenal	Division 1	Away	0-0
8 April	Southampton	FA Cup Rd 6 2R	Spurs	0-5
12 April	Manchester C	Division 1	Away	0-1
13 April	Birmingham C	Division 1	Home	0-2
15 April	Manchester C	Division 1	Home	1-1
18 April	Liverpool	Division 1	Away	2-0
20 April	Burnley	Division 1	Away	0-0
22 April	West ham Utd	Division 1	Away	1-4
30 April	Wolves	Division 1	Home	2-0

N

NEEDHAM, GEORGE

Signed from Shepshed Albion in 1906, George Needham was an outstanding centre-half who never gave less than 100% to the Forest cause. He made his League debut in Forest's last game of the 1905-06 season when the Reds went down 4-1 at Everton! In fact, for the first few years of his Forest career, he had to battle with George Wolfe for a regular first team place.

'Tag' as he came to be known, knew no fear, diving into situations where most centre-halves would avoid and all this despite a slight disability to his left arm. Following the emergence of Joe Mercer, Needham was forced into moving to left-half.

From the start of the 1911-12 season up until the outbreak of war at the end of the 1914-15 campaign, George Needham did not miss a single match. A firm favourite with the Forest crowd, he was appointed club captain just before the outbreak of the hostilities.

NEWPORT COUNTY

Newport County played more matches than any other ex-member of the Football League. In the 61 seasons after they joined the newly formed Third Division in 1920, they played 2,672 games. Champions of the Third Division (South) in 1938-39, they spent just one season in the Second Division.

The two clubs first met in 1946-47, County's first and only season in the Second Division. Forest won the first encounter at the City Ground 6-1 and completed the 'double' by winning 5-2 at Somerton Park with Colin Lyman netting a hat-trick. Newport's only success against Forest came in 1949-50 when they won their home match 4-1, the Reds winning the return 3-0. The clubs last played each other in 1950-51, Forest winning 2-1 at the City Ground and 2-0 away from home.

Newport were promoted from the Fourth Division in 1979-80. They lost their League status automatically after finishing bottom of the Fourth Division in 1987-88.

NEWTON, HENRY

First taken on by Forest in January 1960, he turned professional in June 1961 and made his League debut for the Reds on 8 October 1963 in a 2-0 win over Leicester City at the City Ground. A hard-working half-back, he was forced to play a number of his early games in a Forest shirt at left-back but soon returned to wear the number four shirt, replacing Jeff Whitefoot. He was an ever-present in three seasons including 141 consecutive appearances from 23 November 1963 to 25 March 1967.

Newton was selected for the England Under-23 side in 1964 and was on the verge of selection for the 1970 World Cup squad but never did win a full cap.

After playing in 315 first team games for the Reds, he was allowed to leave the City Ground in October 1970 and joined Everton for £150,000 plus Irish international Tommy Jackson. His time at Goodison Park was hampered by injuries and he only made 83 first team appearances before signing for Derby County in September 1973 for £100,000. Brian Clough' last major signing before he quit, Newton won a League Championship medals with the Rams before moving to end his League career with Walsall in May 1972.

NEUTRAL GROUNDS

The City Ground has been used as a neutral ground for FA Cup matches on a number of occasions and as early as 1905, Aston Villa and Everton played a semi-final there. In the 1996 close season, the City Ground staged the Umbro Cup.

Forest themselves have had to replay on a neutral ground a number of times:

Date	Opponents	Venue	FA Cup	Score
24.03.1885	Queen's Park	Edinburgh	Semi-Final	0-3
28.02.1889	Chatham	The Oval	Round 2	2-3
05.03.1892	West Brom Albion	Molineux	Semi-Final	0-0
09.03.1892	West Brom Albion	Derby	Semi-Final	2-6
24.03.1898	Southampton	Crystal Pal	Semi-final	2-0
28.03.1900	Bury	Bramall Lane	Semi-Final	2-3
22.01.1923	Sheffield United	Meadow Lane	Round 3	1-1
25.01.1923	Sheffield United	Hillsborough	Round 3	0-1
15.03.1926	Bolton Wanderers	Old Trafford	Round 6	0-1
16.01.1946	Watford	Tottenham	Round 3	0-1
23.02.1959	Birmingham City	Filbert St	Round 5	5-0
08.04.1963	Southampton	Tottenham	Round 6	0-5
20.03.1967	Swindon Town	Villa Park	Round 5	3-0
29.01.1973	West Brom Albion	Filbert St	Round 3	1-3
18.03.1974	Newcastle United	Goodison Pk	Round 6	0-0
21.03.1974	Newcastle United	Goodison Pk	Round 6	0-1
18.01.1976	Bristol Rovers	Villa Park	Round 3	6-0

The club's semi-finals were of course played on neutral grounds. In the club's pre-Football League days, Forest were involved in four FA Cup semi-finals. The first of these on 22 March 1879 saw the Reds lose 2-1 to Old Etonians at the Oval. The following season, Forest reached the semi-final stage again, only to lose 1-0 to Oxford University, again at the Oval. In 1884-85, Forest drew 1-1 against Queen's Park at Derby but lost the replay in Edinburgh 3-0. In 1891-92, Forest reached the semi-final stage for the fourth time in 14 seasons only to lose 6-2 to West Bromwich Albion at Derby after the previous two matches had both been drawn.

The full list of Forest's appearances in an FA Cup semi-final on a neutral ground in their League days is as follows:

Date	Opponents	Venue	Score
19.03.1898	Southampton	Bramall Lane	1-1
24.03.1899	Bury	Victoria Ground	1-1
15.03.1902	Southampton	White Hart Lane	1-3
14.03.1959	Aston Villa	Hillsborough	1-0
29.04.1967	Tottenham Hotspur	Hillsborough	1-2
09.04.1988	Liverpool	Hillsborough	1-2
15.04.1989	Liverpool	Hillsborough	0-0*
07.05.1989	Liverpool	Old Trafford	1-3
14.04.1991	West Ham United	Villa Park	4-0

* Match abandoned

The club's appearance in their second FA Charity Shield match against Ipswich Town (5-0 at Wembley on 12 April 1978) and Simod Cup and Zenith Data Systems Cup Finals also qualify, a do the club's FA Cup and League Cup Finals at Crystal Palace and Wembley. The club's two appearances in the European Cup Final were also played on neutral grounds, as was the World Club Championship against National of Uruguay, the match being playedin Tokyo.

NICKNAMES

Many players in the club's history have been fondly known to supporters by their nicknames. One of the first was Arthur 'Sailor' Capes (1896-1902). Signed from Burton Wanderers in the close season of 1896, he scored twice when Forest beat Derby County in the FA Cup Final of 1898.

Known simply as 'The Prince of Inside-forwards', Grenville Morris (1898-1913) was a regular goalscorer during his 15 years at the City Ground and his tally of 199 League goals remains a club record.

Known as 'Tag', George Needham (1905-1915) soon became a firm favourite with the Forest crowd and in the four seasons leading up to the outbreak of World War One was an ever-present.

Forming a great understanding with right-back Walter Dudley, George 'Ginger' Maltby (1906-1914) surprised everyone by just walking straight into the Forest side following his move from Notts Rangers.

Forest goalkeeper Harry Walker (1946-1955) was nicknamed 'Mr Consistency' due to his great anticipation. The club's promotion in 1950-51 had a lot to do with Walker's great goalkeeping.

One of the most popular players ever to grace the City Ground, Joe Baker became an instant hit following his arrival from Arsenal in March 1966 and was nicknamed 'The King'.

Nicknamed 'Spider' because of his long legs, Viv Anderson was the first coloured footballer to play League soccer for the Reds and later the first coloured player to gain a full England cap.

Former Forest captain and England international Stuart Pearce who is now playing with Newcastle United is known by the nickname 'Psycho'

NON-LEAGUE

'Non-League' is the shorthand term for clubs which are not members of the Football League. Nottingham Forest have a very good record against non-League clubs in the FA Cup competition and have never lost a game, though on one occasion, Forest needed a replay to win through. The club's record since the Second World War is:

Date	Opponents	FA Cup	Venue	Score
05.01.1957	Goole Town	Round 3	Home	6-0
10.01.1959	Tooting & Mitcham	Round 3	Away	2-2
24.01.1959	Tooting & Mitcham	Round 3	R Home	3-0

NOTTS COUNTY

Notts County, the oldest League club in the world (founded in 1863) and Nottingham Forest, the third oldest (founded in 1865) enjoy a great rivalry.

It all started in the spring of 1866 when a match billed as the Garibaldis (Forest)v the Lambs (County) took place on the Forest Recreation Ground. The Nottingham Daily Guardian reported the game as a goalless draw, yet according to the earliest Forest club history published in 1891, the Reds won 1-0 courtesy of a goal from W.H. Revis.

When County decided to drop Forest from their fixture list for the 1877-78 campaign, the reason was simply social climbing. The Reds had a more artisan background and did not fit into the gentlemanly pattern of clubs being met by County.

Games did eventually resume between the two clubs, but in dramatic circumstances. The following season they were paired inthe first round of the FA Cup and a crowd of around 500, the biggest for a

Nottingham match at the time saw Forest win 3-1. The Reds reached the semi-finals at the first attempt before losing to the eventual winners, Old Etonians.

In 1880 County resumed ordinary club fixtures with the Reds in an attempt to regain some of their lost prestige but the plan back-fired when Forest won 7-1, a Nottingham 'derby' victory only equalled when the Reds won the County Cup in 1982.

A crowd of over 18,000 witnessed the first League match between the two clubs at Trent Bridge on 8 October 1892 when County won 3-0.

When County opened their present ground on 3 September 1910, it was Forest who provided the opposition. A then record crowd for a Nottingham derby of 27,000 saw a 1-1 draw with Grenville Morris netting for the Reds.

On 13 February 1932, Forest won 6-2 at Meadow Lane with goals from Stocks 3, Heslop, Dent and Singleton.

County's greatest days were in the Tommy Lawton era, late 1947 to early 1952, although the great England centre-forward had 'guested' for the Magpies against Forest at Meadow Lane on 24 April 1943.

During the 1949-50 season, the first-ever Third Division (South) match between the two clubs took place at the City Ground on 3 December 1949. An all-ticket crowd of 38,000 saw Lawton open the scoring in the 27th minute with a powerful header from a Frank Broome corner. In the second-half Broome extended County's lead before Capel pulled one back for Forest. By the time the return game took place, the Magpies were at the top of the table with Forest hard on their heels. County needed to win to clinch promotion. The all-ticket crowd of 46,000 is still the record attendance at Meadow Lane. After an evenly contested first-half, Jackie Sewell headed County ahead and on the hour, Lawton headed a second. It was the first County 'double' over the Reds.

So the Magpies went back to the Second Division and they were followed in 1950-51 by Forest, for whom Wally Ardron scored a club record 36 goals.

When Forest won promotion to the First Division at the end of the 1956-57 season, they were hosts to County in the final match of the campaign. The Magpies who had just saved themselves from relegation put on a magnificent display and beat the Reds 4-2.

The first and so far only Football League Cup meeting between the clubs took place on 25 October 1977 with Forest winning 4-0.

Top flight derbies between the clubs were resumed at Meadow Lane on 24 August 1991 when Forest won 4-0 with goals from Crosby, Charles, Sheringham and Keane. The return at the City Ground on 11 January 1992 finished 1-1 in front of a crowd of 30,168. The end of the campaign saw County relegated, leaving further League derbies in abeyance.

O'KANE, LIAM

Signed from Derry City in December 1968 for £10,000, he made his League debut for Forest in the last game of the 1968-69 season as they went down 1-0 at Leeds United. Unfortunately, O'Kane was injured in that game and it was injuries that were to play an important role in his career.

After succeeding Terry Hennessey as the club's regular centre-half, he won 20 caps for Northern Ireland in his time at the City Ground. In 1971-72 he moved to right-back but broke his leg in the 1-0 win at home to Everton in December. He returned to the Forest side the following season before being an ever-present in 1973-74 as the Reds finished seventh in the Second Division.

A succession of injuries in 1975-76 ended his playing days and in 1977 he joined the club's coaching staff, later becoming reserve and then first team coach. A position he still holds, he is now the club's longest-serving member of staff.

OLDEST

The oldest player to line-up in a Forest first team is Sam Hardy. Sam was 41 years 39 days old when he last turned out for the club in the 1-1 draw at home to Newcastle United on 4 October 1924. Injured during the game, it forced him into retirement.

O'NEILL, MARTIN

Having just won an Irish Cup winners' medal with Distillery in a 3-0

Martin O'Neill – always in the thick of the action.

win over Derry City, he signed for Forest in October 1971. Making his debut as a substitute for John Robertson, O'Neill scored Forest's second goal in a 4-1 win over West Bromwich Albion at the City Ground on 13 November 1971.

He faded somewhat from the Forest first team and at the time of Brian Clough's arrival was languishing in the reserves and on the transfer list. Clough's appointment seemed to transform O'Neill into a tenacious midfield player and he was soon back in the Forest first team. An automatic choice for Northern Ireland, he won 36 caps during his stay at the City Ground. After being disappointed to have been left out of the Reds' 1979 European Cup winning team, he was in the side that beat Hamburg a year later.

After appearing in 371 League and Cup games for Forest and scoring 62 goals, including a hat-trick in the 6-0 win over Chelsea on 28 March 1979, he signed for Norwich City. He helped the Canaries avoid relegation before joining Manchester City in the summer of 1982. After eleven months with the Maine Road club he returned to

Norwich for a second spell, eventually helping them win promotion to the First Division. In 1983 the popular Irishman moved back to Nottingham, but this time to County where unfortunately injury ended his career.

He moved into non-League management with Grantham Town before taking over at Wycombe Wanderers. After later managing Norwich City he took over at Leicester City.

OWN GOALS

When Forest played Tottenham Hotspur in the FA Cup Final of 1991, the game had ended at 1-1 and extra-time was played. After 94 minutes, a Nayim corner was headed on by Paul Stewart and though Des Walker managed to get to the ball before Gary Mabbutt, he only succeeded in heading the ball over Gary Charles on the line and into the roof of the net.

Jim Iley who played 103 League and Cup games for Forest scored an own goal in the match against Bolton Wanderers on 12 November 1960. Peter Grummitt in Forest's goal was making his debut and his first touch of the ball was when picking it out of the back of his net!

One of the occasions when an own goal has worked in Forest's favour came in the club's FA Cup winning year of 1959. The Reds were trailing 2-0 to non-League Tooting and Mitcham with 38 minutes to play when Tooting's Murphy put through his own goal to give the club a lifeline. Billy Gray later converted a penalty and the rest is history!

P

PEACOCK, TOM

A graduate of Nottingham University, he played his early football at Chesterfield, Bath City and Melton Mowbray, where he first attracted the attention of the Forest scouts.

Signing for the Reds in 1933, he made his debut against Oldham Athletic on 9 September that year, scoring Forest's goal in a 3-1 home defeat. He ended that season with seven goals in 15 appearances including four in a 6-1 win over Port Vale.

Over the next two seasons he was the club's top scorer and in 1935-36 scored four goals in a game three times, against Barnsley (Home 6-0); Port Vale (Home 9-2) and Doncaster Rovers (Home 6-2).

A fast and dangerous forward, he scored the last of his six hat-tricks for the club on 5 September 1936 when Forest beat Fulham 5-3 at the City Ground. There is no doubt that if he hadn't had two cartilages removed, which affected his efficiency, he would have played many more games for Forest. His career was ended by the war and he joined the RAF, rising to the rank of flight-sergeant.

He 'guested' for a number of clubs during the Second World War including Chelsea, but when hostilities ended, he became a teacher, later becoming headteacher at St Edmund's Primary School, Mansfield Woodhouse.

PEARCE, STUART

Born in Shepherd's Bush, Stuart Pearce began his footballing career with non-League Wealdstone United when Bobby Gould signed him for Coventry City in October 1983. He played in 51 League games for the Sky Blues before joining Forest in a double deal involving Ian Butterworth in the summer of 1985.

He made his debut for the Reds at Luton Town in the opening game of the 1985-86 season and soon became a firm favourite with the Forest crowd with his aggressive tackling and wholehearted determination. In 1987 he was awarded the first of his 76 England caps and became Forest's captain.

His best season for Forest was 1988-89 when he skippered the Reds to Littlewoods Cup and Simod Cup triumphs.

Pearce, who played in 522 first team games for Forest, scored 88 goals, many of them spectacular efforts from outside the penalty area. A number of his goals also came from the penalty spot, though he will be remembered for failing from the twelve-yard mark in the semi-final penalty shoot-out against West Germany in the 1990 World Cup. However, he had a superb Euro '96 and laid the ghost to rest by scoring twice from the spot in penalty shoot-outs before announcing his retirement from international football at the end of the tournament.

However, he became the first manager to represent his country when he was persuaded to play in England's World Cup qualifiers in 1996-97. Pearce was asked to become Forest's player-manager follow-

Stuart Pearce, heading clear in the game against Queen's Park Rangers.

ing Frank Clark's departure in December 1996. The following month Pearce won the Manager of the Month award and though he initially led the club out of the relegation zone, the season ended with the club dropping into the First Division.

One of the most popular players ever to wear the red of Nottingham Forest, he left the club in the summer of 1997 to join Newcastle United for whom he played in 25 Premier League games in 1997-98.

PENALTIES

The scorer of the club's first penalty in the Football League was John MacPherson who netted from the spot in Forest's 4-3 defeat at home to West Bromwich Albion.

During the Division One match between Nottingham Forest and Bolton Wanderers on Boxing Day 1924, Forest were awarded a penalty. At the time, Harry Martin, the club's regular penalty taker was in the dressing-room receiving attention from the trainer. Forest refused to take the kick until Martin was summoned from the treatment room and when he did appear he scored to enable Forest to draw 1-1.

Forest 'keeper Mark Crossley saved Gary Linekers's penalty in the 1991 FA Cup Final against Tottenham Hotspur.

Stuart Pearce, Forest's most capped player with 76 caps will always be remembered for failing from the spot in the 1990 World Cup semi-final shoot-out against West Germany although he did score twice in penalty shoot-outs in Euro '96.

Forest's leading scorer from the spot is John Robertson who scored 47 penalties during his 514 first team appearances.

PITCH

The City Ground pitch is one of the biggest in the Premier League and measures 116 yards by 76 yards.

PLASTIC

There have been four Football League clubs that have replaced their normal grass playing pitches with artificial surfaces at one stage or another. Queen's Park Rangers were the first in 1981 but the Loftus Road plastic was discarded in 1988 in favour of a return to turf. Luton Town (1985), Oldham Athletic and Preston North End (both 1986) followed.

Though Forest never played on the Deepdale plastic and only once on Oldham Athletic's Boundary Park plastic, where they lost 2-1, they have been regular visitors to Queen's Park Rangers and Luton Town. The first time they played on the Loftus Road plastic on 11 February 1984, a Garry Birtles goal gave them a 1-0 win, their only success in six League and Cup visits. Forest were Luton's opponents the first time they played on their plastic, a Neil Webb goal giving the Reds a 1-1 draw. Forest's only victory in seven games on the Kenilworth Road plastic came in 1988-89 when two goals from Nigel Clough, one a penalty, and another from Garry Parker gave the Reds a 3-2 win.

PLATTS, LARRY

One of the most unluckiest players ever to play for Forest, Larry Platts played the game of his life in the fourth round of the FA Cup as the

Garry Parker, hero of the plastic pitch in 1988-89. Garry is seen here in the colours of Leicester City.

Reds beat Manchester United 2-0 in a game played at Maine Road because Old Trafford was still being repaired after suffering bomb damage.

His only other appearance in that 1946-47 season was in a 6-0 win over Southampton three days later. He should have played in the following match at Luton but missed his train from Brighton where he was stationed! Unfortunately injury robbed Forest of Platts for the rest of the season.

POINTS

Under the three points for a win system which was introduced in 1981-82, Forest' best points tally is the 94 points gained in 1997-98 when the club finished top of the First Division. The club's best points haul under the old two points for a win system was 70 points from 46 matches in 1950-51 when the club won the Third Division (South) championship. It would have netted the club 100 points under the present method.

The worst record under either system was the meagre 23 points in 1913-14 though that was from a 38-match programme. The lowest total from a programme of 42 matches was the 24 points in 1924-25 when the club were relegated from the First Division.

POSTPONED

The bleak winter of 1962-63 described at the time as the 'Modern Ice Age' proved to be one of the most chaotic seasons in British soccer.

The worst Saturday for League action in that awful winter was 9 February when only seven Football League fixtures went ahead.

The worst Saturday for the FA Cup was 5 January, the day of the third round, when only three of the 32 ties could be played.

Nottingham Forest v Wolverhampton Wanderers had to be postponed five times and was eventually played on 29 January with Forest winning 4-3 in front of a 38,580 crowd.

Other Forest games have been postponed due to fog, snow, ice, flooding and because their opponents had International commitments.

PREMIER LEAGUE

The sales of Des Walker and Darren Wassall in the summer of 1992 were never plugged by Brian Clough and this caused great concern among many supporters as the season started for Nottingham Forest. But a 1-0 win over Liverpool in front of the Sky Sports cameras on the opening day of the season seemed to calm the nerves. However, the scorer of that winning goal, Teddy Sheringham was soon on his way to Tottenham Hotspur and as the goals dried up, they were soon conceded and in the end Forest's good football was never enough to keep them in the top flight and they finished bottom of the League.

Having regained their place in the Premiership at the first attempt under Frank Clark, Forest strengthened their squad with the £2.9 million signing of Dutch international Bryan Roy from Foggia. The club made a flying start to the season with an eleven match unbeaten run which took them to second place in the table. However, the side then went five games without a goal. The year ended with Forest in inconsistent form but then they hit such a rich vein of form that no side in the Premiership could hope to match. They won nine games out of ten including a 7-1 demolition of Sheffield Wednesday at Hillsborough to finish the season in third place.

Having re-established themselves as a force in the Premiership, Forest were hoping to improve even further on last season's performance in 1995-96. They started the campaign with a 4-3 win at Southampton and then went 12 League games without defeat before losing 7-0 at Blackburn Rovers. Unfortunately in what was a very demanding nine months, the club failed to qualify for Europe again and finished the season in ninth place.

By mid-November in the 1996-97 season, Forest had slumped to the foot of the table and the following month, manager Frank Clark called it a day. Stuart Pearce took over the position of player-manager and led the club out of the bottom three for the first time in three months. However, Forest then failed to score in five of their next six matches and after Southampton gained a rare away win in April, Forest's fate was as good as sealed and they ended the season at the foot of the table, five points adrift of Middlesborough in 19th place.

PRISON WARDERS

Former Nottingham Forest defenders Bobby McKinlay (1951-1969) and Doug Fraser (1970-1972) had spent their footballing careers trying to keep opponents out. They became prison warders in Nottingham, where they were required to keep them in!

PROMOTION

Nottingham Forest have won promotion seven times. Having suffered relegation for the first time in 1905-06, they returned to the First Division as champions of the Second Division the following year with the following record:

P.	W.	D.	L.	F.	A.	Pts
38	28	4	6	74	36	60

Relegated again at the end of the 1910-11 season, the Reds didn't win promotion until 1921-22 when they virtually ran away with the Second Division title:

P.	W.	D.	L.	F.	A.	Pts
42	22	12	8	51	30	56

Two years later they were back in the Second Division and after spending 17 seasons there, were relegated to the Third Division (South) for the first time in their history. Forest won promotion in only their second season in the lower division, sprinting away with the title in 1950-51. They were six points ahead of runners-up Norwich City and 13 points ahead of the third placed club:

P.	W.	D.	L.	F.	A.	Pts
46	30	10	6	110	40	70

Forest won promotion for a fourth time in 1956-57 when they finished as runners-up to Leicester City in the Second Division. The club were now back in the First Division after an absence of 32 years:

P.	W.	D.	L.	F.	A.	Pts
42	22	10	10	94	55	54

Forest spent 15 seasons in the top flight before relegation to the Second Division in 1971-72. They won promotion in 1976-77, ending their League season in third place, four points ahead of Bolton Wanderers who still had three games to play. The Trotters failed to overtake the Reds who won promotion in third place. However, they won the League Championship the following season:

P.	W.	D.	L.	F.	A.	Pts
42	21	10	11	77	43	52

Relegated in 1992-93 after finishing bottom of the Premier League, Forest won promotion the next season. Embarking on a 13 game unbeaten run, they lost just one of their last 16 matches to finish as runners-up to long-term leaders, Crystal Palace:

P.	W.	D.	L.	F.	A.	Pts
46	23	14	9	74	49	83

After relegation in 1996-97, Forest won the First Division championship at the first attempt, thus returning to the Premier League after just one season out of the top flight. The club's total of 94 points was the biggest haul in its history:

P.	W.	D.	L.	F.	A.	Pts
46	28	10	8	82	42	94

PUGH, BOB

Cardiff-born Bob Pugh began his footballing career with Symonds Yat before signing as an amateur with Newport County. He later played with Bury before joining Forest in 1931.

A naturally left-sided player, he made his League debut for the Reds at Stoke City on 17 January 1931, playing at inside-left. However, it was as a half-back that the Welshman became a first team regular, forming part of the famous Forest half-back line of McKinlay, Graham and Pugh.

He played for Forest until 1938 when a serious injury suffered against West Ham United ended his career, though he did play in the second game of the 1938-39 season.

After his playing days were over, he continued his association with the City Ground when becoming a scout.

QUICKEST GOAL

It is an impossible task to state accurately the club's quickest goalscorer. Whilst there have probably been quicker goals, Arthur Shaw's goal in the opening seconds of Forest's FA Cup tie at Clapton on 17 January 1891 certainly opened the floodgates as Forest recorded their highest-ever first-class win.

QUIGLEY, JOHNNY

Glasgow-born Johnny Quigley began his footballing career with Celtic before being released. He joined Nottingham Forest in July 1957 from Ashfield Juniors and made his League debut on 5 October 1957 at White Hart Lane, scoring the winner in a thrilling 4-3 win for the Reds.

On 8 November 1958 he became the first Forest player to score a post-war First Division hat-trick as the Reds beat Manchester City 4-0 at the City Ground. He was the scorer of some vital goals for Forest, perhaps none more so than the one against Aston Villa at Hillsborough in the FA Cup semi-final of 1959.

After scoring 58 goals in 270 first team appearances, he left the City Ground to join Huddersfield Town. From there he signed for Bristol City and later captained the Ashton Gate club. In July 1968 he joined Mansfield Town and as captain inspired the Stags to two superb FA Cup runs. After being appointed assistant-manager to Jock Basford at Field Mill, he was dismissed in November 1971 and went to coach in the Middle East.

RAPID SCORING

When Gillingham returned to the Football League in 1950-51 after a 12-year absence, they were given a lesson in finishing as Forest beat them 9-2 at the City Ground. At half-time, the Reds were leading 6-1, all the goals coming in a period of 35 minutes.

Tommy Capel opened the scoring after nine minutes and added a second eleven minutes later following a one-two between Bill Morley and Tucker Johnson. Capel completed his hat-trick in the 27th minute after dribbling through a static Gillingham defence. Three minutes later, Wally Ardron hit home an unstoppable drive from the edge of the area before Veck headed home a goal for the visitors. Capel hit his fourth and Forest's fifth in the 41st minute and then just a minute before half-time, Ardron headed home a sixth goal. Forest's scorers in the second-half were Johnson 2 and Ardron.

RECEIPTS

The club's record receipts are £272,735 for the FA Cup third round replay against Sheffield Wednesday on 19 January 1994. The British record is £2,016,000 paid by the 80,000 fans who watched the 1991 FA Cup Final between Nottingham Forest and Tottenham Hotspur. Including television fees, that figure is increased to nearly £3 million.

RECORDS

League Points	94	(Division One 1997-98)
Goals	110	(Division Three South 1950-51)
Win	14-0	(v Clapton FA Cup 1890-91)
Goals Aggregate	199	(Grenville Morris 1898-1913)
Individual Goals	36	(Wally Ardron 1950-51)
League Appearances	614	(Bobby McKinlay 1951-70)
Capped Player	76	(Stuart Pearce 1987-1997)

RE-ELECTION

After relegation to the Second Division in 1911, Forest suffered the indignity of re-election in 1913-14 after finishing bottom of the League with the following record:

P.	W.	D.	L.	F.	A.	Pts
38	7	9	22	37	76	23

The club's heaviest defeat in that season came at Leeds City when the Reds were beaten 8-0.

RELEGATION

Nottingham Forest have suffered the anguish of relegation on seven occasions. The Reds suffered relegation for the first time in 1906 but they returned from the Second Division as champions the following year. Forest went down again in 1911 but it was 1921-22 before they returned to the top flight, again as champions.

The Reds survived two seasons in the First Division but then suffered relegation a third time in 1925. During the late 1930s, the club teetered on the brink of relegation and though there was a slight improvement after the war, the club finished next to bottom in 1949 and fell into the Third Division (South) for the first time in their history.

After promotion to the Second Division in 1950-51 and then to the First Division in 1956-57, Forest had 15 seasons in the top flight before being relegated for a fifth time in 1972. Promoted five seasons later, the club were relegated for a sixth time when they finished bottom of the Premier League in 1992-93. The club's last experience of relegation came in 1996-97 when the Reds again finished bottom of the Premier League, five points adrift of Middlesborough who were deducted three points for failing to fulfil a fixture.

RICHARDSON, PAUL

A talented schoolboy footballer, he signed for the Reds as an apprentice professional in August 1966 and after impressing in the club's junior sides, signed full-time professional forms two years later.

An England Youth international, he made his Forest debut against Sunderland at Roker Park on 4 November 1967 coming on for Bobby McKinlay. His first starting appearance came in the final game of that 1967-68 season when Forest lost 6-1 at Liverpool!

A loyal servant to the City Ground club, the Shirebrook-born player never quite fulfilled his early promise and often had to be content with playing in a number of unfamiliar positions. After appearing in 248 League and Cup games for Forest, scoring 21 goals he left the City Ground in October 1976 for Chester but by the end of that season he had joined Stoke City.

He played the best football of his career at the Victoria Ground, appearing in 127 League games before later playing for Sheffield United, Blackpool, Swindon Town and Swansea City.

RITCHIE, ARCHIE

Kirkaldy-born Archie Ritchie made a name for himself with East Stirling, eventually winning an international cap against Wales in 1891. Signing for Forest at the end of that year, he partnered Adam Scott to begin the Forest tradition of long-serving full-back partnerships. Having made the first team debut during the FA Cup run of 1891-92, he made his League debut for Forest in the 4-3 defeat at home by Stoke on 10 September 1892.

Paul Richardson, one of the club's most versatile players.

Standing only 5ft 6ins, an inch higher than Scott, they formed probably the smallest full-back pairing in Football League history.

A bad injury in the FA Cup semi-final win over Southampton threatened to keep him out of Forest's 1898 FA Cup Final with Derby County but happily he recovered to take his place in the Forest side which won 3-1.

Playing the last of his 178 League and Cup games for Forest in 1899, he became a noted bowls player with another former Forest player, Bob Norris.

ROBERTSON, JOHN

John Robertson's career had its roots in a nursery team by the name of Drumchapel Amateurs, which also has a claim to fame in the production of two other famous Scottish internationals in John Wark and Asa Hartford. He had gained Scottish Schoolboy and Youth honours before he came south of the border to join Forest in May 1970.

It wasn't until the dual arrival of Brian Clough and Peter Taylor that Robertson's talent began to be harnessed to its best advantage. The pair encouraged him to do his own thing, be individualistic, hug the touchline, demand the ball at his feet and wait for him to do the rest.

He gained the first of 28 full Scottish caps against Northern Ireland in 1978 and won several honours during Forest's glory years. He played a prominent part in Forest's two remarkable European Cup successes in consecutive years. For in the first final against Malmo in Munich, it was his long cross, which winged its way over the goal to the far post for Trevor Francis to score the only goal. Twelve months later in Madrid, it was Robertson's incursion into Hamburg's penalty area on his right foot, which produced the only goal and kept the top European trophy in this country.

He continued to serve Forest until the summer of 1983 when he left to join Peter Taylor at the Baseball Ground for £135,000, a fee set by a tribunal. Unfortunately the winger had to undergo a cartilage operation in his first season at Derby and two years later returned to the City Ground. However, his old magic had deserted him and he moved into non-League football with Corby Town, then Stamford and Grantham.

Most full-backs who figured they knew how to handle the mercurial attacker went into the game assured that Robertson would in-

John Robertson

variably be at his most dangerous when he cut inside. What they didn't know was exactly when he was going to do it and that is what made John Robertson lethal.

RUNNERS-UP

Nottingham Forest have finished runners-up in a Football League season on four occasions – 1956-7 (Division Two); 1966-67 (Division One); 1978-79 (Division One) and 1993-94 (Division One).

S

SCOTT, ADAM

One of the least well-known group of Scotsmen who joined Nottingham Forest after their disastrous season of 1889-90, he signed for them from Coatbridge Albion.

Standing only 5ft 5ins, he more than made up for his lack of inches with great determination and tenacity. He made his Football League debut for Forest in the opening match of the 1892-93 season when they drew 2-2 at Everton, though he played in a number of FA Cup games prior to this.

Forming a highly successful full-back partnership with Archie Ritchie, he was voted Forest's best player in their 1898 FA Cup Final victory over Derby County at the Crystal Palace.

After playing the last of his 210 League and Cup games on 4 November 1899, he decided to retire. There were worries within the club that the diminutive full-back would never be adequately replaced but fortunately Jim Iremonger was waiting in the wings.

SCOTT, FREDDIE

Born in Fatfield, County Durham, Freddie Scott played his early football with Bradford and Bolton Wanderers but when the game resumed after the Second World War, he was with York City.

The diminutive winger was signed by Forest in September 1946 and went straight into the team that played Newport County at the City Ground. His silky skills created five of Forest's goals in their 6-1 win. A fast, direct winger, he was a beautiful crosser of the ball and when Wally Ardron joined the Reds in 1949, it seemed as if the majority of his goals came from Freddie Scott's crosses. However, he wasn't just a creator of goals and in his ten years at the City Ground, he scored 46 goals in 322 League and Cup appearances.

Freddie Scott also holds the record for the oldest outfield player to turn out for Forest in a first team match, having appeared against Rotherham United at Millmoor on 15 September 1956, just twenty days short of his 40th birthday.

SECOND DIVISION

Nottingham Forest have had five spells in the Second Division. Suffering relegation for the first time in 1906, the club returned to the top flight as Second Division champions the following year. Forest went down again in 1911 and three years later had to apply for re-election after finishing bottom of the Second Division. Just before the start of the 1921-22 season, Forest signed goalkeeper Sam Hardy and Noah Burton from Derby County. The result was devastating as the Reds again won the Second Division championship.

In fact, promotion for the club had perhaps come a little too soon, for after just two seasons in the top flight, the club were back in the Second Division for a third spell. The Reds spent 17 seasons in the Second Division, mostly in mid-table before relegation to the Third Division (South) in 1949. Promoted after two seasons, Forest almost went straight into the First Division, finishing just two points adrift of promoted Cardiff City. In 1956-57, Forest began the season in fine form, winning five of their first six matches and continued this good form throughout the season to gain promotion as runners-up to Leicester City.

Relegated in 1971-72, Forest's fifth and final spell in the Second Division saw them spend five seasons there before winning promotion in 1976-77.

SEMI-FINALS

Up to the end of the 1997-98 season, Nottingham Forest had been involved in 12 FA Cup semi-finals and six Football League Cup semi-finals as well as appearing in that stage of the following competitions - European Cup, UEFA Cup, Anglo-Scottish Cup, Simod Cup and Zenith Data Systems Cup.

SHERINGHAM, TEDDY

He joined Millwall as an apprentice in June 1982 before graduating through the club's junior sides and making his League debut in January 1984. In 1986-87 he was an ever-present, scoring 18 goals and in 1987-88 missed only one game as the Lions roared their way into the top flight for the first time in their history as Second Division champions.

Teddy Sheringham, seen here in the colours of Tottenham Hotspur.

After two seasons, the Lions found themselves back in Division Two and although they failed at the play-off stage, Sheringham had ca magnificent season, scoring 33 League goals, including all four in the 4-1 win over Plymouth Argyle.

In July 1991 he signed for Nottingham Forest for £2 million. He was not an unqualified success in his first season at the City Ground despite playing in all but three games of Forest's 60-match programme and topping the scoring lists with 22 League and Cup goals. The highlights of his season were a hat-trick against Crystal Palace in a fifth round League Cup tie and his first two appearances at Wembley, the first as a winner in the Zenith Cup Final against Southampton and then as a loser against Manchester United in the League Cup Final.

He kicked off the 1992-93 season with a goal against Liverpool but two games later he had signed for Tottenham Hotspur. He finished that season with 29 goals and won the Premier League 'Golden Boot' award. He also gained his first international cap in a 1-1 draw against Poland and has now represented his country on 35 occasions. He went on to score 96 goals for Spurs in 197 League and Cup games before joining Manchester United for a fee of £3.5 million in June 1997.

SHILTON, PETER

Undoubtedly one of the greatest goalkeepers of the modern era, he made his Football League debut for Leicester City as a 16-year-old and progressed to the point where he put manager Matt Gillies under pressure to either play him at the expense of Gordon Banks or let him go.

In November 1974 after he had made 286 League appearances for the Filbert Street club, he joined Stoke City for £325,000, a world record fee for a goalkeeper. However, following the club's relegation in 1976-77 he played in three Division Two matches before being transferred to Nottingham Forest. Making his debut in the 2-0 home win over Aston Villa on 17 September 1977, he went on to keep 23 clean sheets as Forest won the League Championship.

At the City Ground under Brian Clough he also won two European Cup winners' medals, a League Cup winners' and runners-up medal and a European Super Cup medal. In 1978 he was selected as the PFA Player of the Year and won the first of his 19 caps he gained whilst at the City Ground.

Unfortunate to have been around at the same time as Ray Clemence

Peter Shilton, producing yet another breathtaking save.

who played 61 times for England, the number of caps he might have won, had he been unchallenged, might have spiralled towards the 200 mark. As it was, Shilton became England's most capped player with 125 international appearances to his name.

He left Forest in 1982 after playing in 272 League and Cup games to join Southampton for £300,000 and moved to Derby County in 1987. He later became player-manager of Plymouth Argyle before playing in a couple of games in Bolton Wanderers promotion-winning season of 1994-95. He had a spell on the staff of West Ham United before ending his League career with Leyton Orient.

Awarded the MBE, no player in the game's history has appeared in more Football League matches than 'Shilts'.

SHIN PAD

The shin-pad was invented by Sam Widdowson, Nottingham Forest's all-round sportsman in 1874. These were modified cricket pads to protect his shins from the rather unsporting tactic of 'hacking' (kicking shins).

SIMOD CUP

The Simod Cup replaced the Full Members' Cup for the 1987-88 season. Forest's first match in the competition saw them go down 2-1 at Elm Park to Second Division Reading. However, in 1988-89, Forest more than made amends. They beat Chelsea 4-1 at Stamford Bridge with Chapman, Gaynor, Pearce and Parker netting for Forest and then defeated Ipswich Town at Portman Road 3-1 with Hodge, Pearce and Crosby getting on the scoresheet. Drawn at home against Crystal Palace in the semi-final, Forest triumphed 3-1 with Neil Webb scoring two of the goals and Stuart Pearce his third in three successive Simod Cup games.

Facing Everton in the Final at Wembley, two goals apiece from Gary Parker and Lee Chapman gave Forest a 4-3 win in front of a 46,606 crowd.

SMITH, HARRY

Signed from Throckley Athletic in 1928, the Newcastle-born fullback found it almost impossible to break into Forest's Football League side due to the consistency shown by Jimmy Barrington and Billy Thompson. After making his debut in a goalless draw against Chelsea at the City Ground on 28 December 1929, his chief role became one of cover for any of the club's defensive positions.

In one run of 18 consecutive appearances in 1930-31 he appeared in four different positions. He finally became a first-team regular in 1934-35, initially at right-back and then at centre-half as a replacement for the England international Tommy Graham.

He served the club for almost nine years before being released at the end of the 1936-37 season. During that time he played in 169 League and Cup games, with his one and only goal coming in a 2-1 win at home to Port Vale in the 1931-32 season.

SOUTH SHIELDS

Joining the Second Division as South Shields Athletic in 1919, they subsequently dropped the word Athletic from their name and in 1930-31, the club moved to Gateshead and adopted their new name.

Meeting for the first time on 8 November 1919, the clubs played out a goalless draw at the City Ground before South Shields won their home match 5-2 with Bert Davis scoring both Forest goals. Though Forest lost 2-1 at home the following season, they won their next four meetings at the City Ground against South Shields culminating in a 7-2 win on 3 September 1927. When the two clubs last met later that season, Forest triumphed 4-3 in the north-east with Wadsworth and Stocks scoring two goals apiece.

Relegated at the end of that 1927-28 season, they spent the rest of their time in the lower divisions.

SPAVEN, JACK

He began his footballing career with Goole Town just before the First World War when working at the docks in the town. During the hostilities Spaven served with the Royal Horse Artillery in France and was awarded the Military Medal.

After the war he joined Scunthorpe United before signing for Forest in 1920. Making his debut for the Reds at home to Birmingham, he scored in Forest's 2-1 defeat. He was Forest's leading goalscorer in his first three seasons with the club and hit a hat-trick in Forest's 6-1 Christmas Day victory over Rotherham in 1920.

Famed for his powerful shooting with either foot, the City Ground faithful were encouraged to shout 'Shoot Spav' whenever the Scarborough-born forward was in sight of goal.

After scoring 50 goals in his 170 League and Cup games, he left Forest in 1926 to play for Grantham Town, where he later took over a public house.

SPONSORS

Nottingham Forest's sponsors are Pinnacle Insurance plc, though over the years the club's other sponsors have included Labatt's, Skol and Shipstones Ales.

SPOUNCER, ALF

After playing his early football with his home-town club Gainsborough Trinity, he joined Sheffield United before signing for Forest in May 1897.

Playing his first game for the Reds in a friendly against Gainsborough Trinity, he settled into the left-wing position and made his

League debut against Notts County in the opening game of the 1897-98 season. At the end of that season he had gained an FA Cup winners' medal, following Forest's 3-1 win over Derby County.

He won an England cap in March 1890 when they beat Wales 3-1 at Wrexham and a Second Division Championship medal with Forest in 1906-07. He scored a hat-trick in Forest's 12-0 win over Leicester Fosse in April 1909 but after scoring 52 goals in 336 League and Cup games, he went to coach in Europe, including a spell at Barcelona. The last surviving member of Forest's 1898 Cup-winning side, he died in August 1962, aged 85.

STOCKS, CYRIL

Born in Pinxton, Derbyshire in 1905, Cyril Stocks played his early football with South Normanton Amateurs and South Normanton Colliery before being persuaded to sign for Nottingham Forest in 1923.

After impressing in the reserves, he was given his Leagued debut at home to Newcastle United on 4 October 1924. When Jack Spaven left the City Ground in 1926, Stocks took his chance at inside-forward and linked up well on the left-wing with Syd Gibson.

Though not a prolific goalscorer, he did score three hat-tricks in his time with the club - Reading (Home 5-0 on 22 February 1930); Oldham Athletic (Home 4-1 on 27 September 1930) and Notts County (Away 6-2 on 13 February 1932).

Although somewhat injury prone, he kept his place at inside-right until 1934, playing his last game against Fulham in April, after having scored 80 goals in his 257 first team appearances.

STOREY-MOORE, IAN

He signed professional forms for the Reds in May 1961 after being spotted playing in Scunthorpe junior football. He made his League debut on 10 May 1963 as Forest beat Ipswich Town 2-1 at the City Ground. However, after that it took a little time for him to become a first team regular.

A brilliant, exciting player, Storey-Moore was a lethal finisher and was the club's top scorer in 1966-67, 1968-69, 1969-70, 1970-71 and 1971-72, even though he left the club in February 1972!

His best season was 1966-67 when he scored 25 League and Cup

Ian Storey-Moore

goals including a hat-trick in a 3-2 defeat of Everton in an FA Cup sixth round tie. His other hat-trick for the club came in March 1971 as Crystal Palace were beaten 3-1.

There is no doubt if it hadn't been for Alf Ramsey's policy of not playing wingers, Storey-Moore would have won more than the one England cap he gained against Holland in 1970. After scoring 118 League and Cup goals in 272 games he joined Manchester United, although he almost moved to Derby County - the Rams even introduced him to the crowd as their new player!

An instant hit at Old Trafford, he had only played in 39 League games when injuries forced him to retire. He later made a number of appearances for Chicago Stings in the NASL and played for and managed both Shepshed Charterhouse and Burton Albion.

SUBSTITUTES

Substitutes were first allowed in the Football League in season 1965-66. The first appearance of a substitute in League football came at Burnden Park when Charlton Athletic's Keith Peacock came on during Bolton's 4-2 win.

Forest's first substitute was Barry McArthur who came on for Colin Addison on 4 September 1965 in a 2-1 defeat against Leeds United at Elland Road. Forest's first goalscoring substitute was David Wilson who scored in the 5-0 win over West Ham United at the City Ground on 16 October 1965.

The greatest number of substitutes used in a single season by Forest under the single substitute rule was 32 in 1968-69 but since 1986-87 two substitutes were allowed and in 1993-94 the club used 43 in 46 matches. Over the past few seasons three substitutes have been allowed and in 1997-98, the club used 72.

The greatest number of substitute appearances for Forest in the

Football League have been made by Phil Starbuck and Jason Lee who both came on during 27 games with 12 and 6 more appearances in cup-ties respectively.

It was in 1994-95 that Jason Lee caused the club to re-write its record books on the matter with an extraordinary 17 League appearances in the number 12 shirt.

On 25 February 1991, Nottingham Forest substitute Nigel Jemson was called upon to replace the injured Steve Hodge in a fifth round FA Cup tie at Southampton. As he peeled off his tracksuit top, he discovered that he had left his shirt in the dressing-room. He had to use the shirt of the other substitute Ian Woan!

SUNDAY FOOTBALL

The first ever Sunday matches in the Football League took place on 20 January 1974 during the three-day week imposed by the government during its trial of strength with the coalminers. On that Sunday Forest lost 2-1 at Preston North End with Duncan McKenzie scoring for the Reds. Forest had in fact played Bristol Rovers in the third round of the FA Cup on 6 January, winning 4-3 with goals from Martin 2, Lyall (pen) and Chapman. The first Sunday League game at the City Ground was played on 3 March 1974 when neighbour Notts County forced a goalless draw.

Many of Forest's triumphs have also come on a Sunday - the Football League Cup final appearances against Luton Town (3-1 on 9 April 1989); Oldham Athletic (1-0 on 30 April 1990) and Manchester United (0-1 on 12 April 1992) and the Zenith Data Systems Cup win over Everton (4-3 on 30 April 1989).

SUSPENSIONS

Though he was not with Nottingham Forest at the time, Enoch West who had topped the First Division goalscoring charts in 1907-08 was suspended in 191.

He was found guilt along with other players of helping to 'fix' a game involving his new club Manchester United and Liverpool. His suspension was the longest in Football League history and he was banned for 30 years, his 'life' sentence being lifted in November 1945.

SUSTAINED SCORING

During the 1956-57 Second Division promotion winning season, Forest put together a run of seven successive victories including two successive 7-1 wins against Port Vale and Barnsley. In a remarkable run of 16 games, Jim Barratt scored in 14 of them, netting a total of 20 goals. He ended the season with 27 goals in 32 League appearances.

SUTTON, STEVE

After progressing through the junior ranks at Forest, he made his first team debut for the Reds in a 1-1 draw at Norwich City on 25 October 1980.

However, due to Peter Shilton's brilliant consistency, the Derby-born goalkeeper found his first team opportunities somewhat limited. He was loaned out to Mansfield Town and even played for the Stags against Forest in a County Cup match. After Shilton's departure, Sutton claimed the first team goalkeeper's jersey but Brian Clough still signed Dutchman Hans van Breukelen. Midway through the 1984-85 season, Sutton found himself in Forest's reserve side.

After impressing in Forest's Second XI he was rewarded with promotion as the club's first choice 'keeper in 1986. One of the best uncapped goalkeepers in the country, he lost his place to Mark Crossley at the end of the 1989-90 season and later joined Derby County.

T

TELEVISION

Nottingham Forest have of course appeared on television on many occasions including FA Cup Finals and European matches but first appeared on 'Match of the Day' on 17 October 1964 when they lost 3-2 at Leicester City with Crowe and Wignall scoring Forest's goals.

Roy Dwight the scorer of Forest's first goal when they beat Luton Town 2-1 in the 1959 FA Cup Final was forced to watch the second-half on television from a hospital bed after being carried off with a broken leg.

Brian Clough has appeared on television a number of times and on one occasion planted a kiss on the cheeks of a journalist at the end of a televised football match in front of millions of viewers!

TEXACO CUP

The predecessor of the Anglo-Scottish Cup, it was launched in 1970-71 and was for English, Irish and Scottish club sides not involved in European competitions that season.

Forest's first match in the competition saw them drawn against Airdrieonians but despite goals from Cormack and Storey-Moore they could only draw their home leg 2-2. A similar scoreline in Scotland led to a penalty shoot-out which Forest lost 5-2 to go out of the competition in the first round.

THIRD DIVISION

Forest were relegated to the Third Division for the first time in their history at the end of the 1948-49 season.

The club's first game in the Third Division saw them draw 2-2 at Brighton with Wally Ardron scoring Forest's equalising goal. The former Rotherham United centre-forward had been signed during the summer and though he was to score 25 goals that season, it wasn't enough to win promotion for the Reds who finished fourth and had to watch Notts County take the championship.

In 1950-51, Forest ran away with the title, their closest rivals being Norwich City, who were some six points adrift of the Reds. It was a season in which the clubs et new divisional records - 70 points and 110 goals scored. Wally Ardron broke Dave 'Boy' Martin's club goalscoring record with 36 goals including hat-tricks in the wins over Aldershot (Home 7-0); Gillingham (Home 9-2) and Gillingham (Away 4-1).

THOMAS, GEOFF

Derby-born Geoff Thomas had represented Derbyshire Schools before joining Forest during the Second World War. He made his debut for the Reds as a 17-year-old in a 2-0 win over Walsall on 25 March 1944.

His League debut came in the opening game of the 1946-47 season at right-Back in a 3-2 defeat at Barnsley. Unlucky with injuries, he often found it difficult to get back into the side due to the outstanding performances of Bill Whare and Jack Hutchinson and so in 1950-51 he moved to left-back. During that season he missed only one game as Forest won the Third Division (South) championship. In 1954 he represented the FA and in 1956-57 he was an important member of Forest's promotion-winning side.

His one and only goal for the club came in a 2-0 win over Leicester City in August 1955 and though by the time Forest went to Wembley in 1959 he had lost his place to Joe McDonald, he travelled as reserve. He played the last of his 431 League and Cup games for Forest in April 1960, thus ending 16 years' superb service. Immediately following his departure from the City Ground, he became player-manager at Bourne Town.

THOMPSON, BILL

Born in Derby in 1900, Bill Thompson won an England Schoolboys cap before starting work as a draughtsman at the local Rolls-Royce factory during World War One. Discovered playing for Royce's much respected works side, he was signed by Forest in 1922 as cover for Harry Jones and Harry Bulling.

He made his Leagued debut at right-back in the opening game of the 1922-23 season when Forest beat Sunderland 1-0. Forming a fine partnership with Percy Barratt, he went on to play in 390 League and Cup games for Forest, scoring five goals, all from the penalty spot.

Thompson was a popular choice as club captain when he took over from Bob Wallace in 1930. A determined and rugged full-back, he played his last game for the club on 6 April 1935 in a 2-2 draw against Manchester United at the City Ground before retiring.

TOURS

Nottingham Forest's first overseas tour was undertaken in the close season of 1905 when they went to Argentina. They had a successful trip, recording seven wins: Rosarinos 5-0; Belgrano 7-0; Britanicos 13-1; Rosarinos 6-0; Alumni 6-0; Argentinos 5-0 and Ligo Argentina 9-1. Unfortunately Forest were relegated to Division Two at the end of the following season!

TRANSFERS

Forest's first-ever six-figure fee was for Jim Baxter from Sunderland in 1967 though the move turned out to be a huge disappointment.

In 1972 Matt Gillies the then manager of Nottingham Forest was the first to sell four players for over £100,000 - Terry Hennessey went to Derby County for £110,000 in 1970; Henry Newton to Everton in 1970 for £130,000, Ian Storey-Moore to Manchester United in 1972 for £120,000 and Peter Cormack to Liverpool in 1972 for £110,000. The Forest manager later tended his resignation, much to the relief of the Forest fans!

On 10 February 1979, the day after Forest had signed Trevor Francis for £1.15 million - officially the first seven-figure fee for a player - he played for the 'A' team at Notts County in front of a crowd of 40. Afterwards the FA said he was not properly registered and the Football League said they had not received the player's registration.

The record transfer fee the club has received is £8.5 million from Liverpool for Stan Collymore in June 1995. Forest's record transfer fee paid is £4.5 million to Celtic for Pierre van Hooijdonk in March 1997.

U

UEFA CUP

Formerly known as the Fairs Cup, its name was changed in 1971 when it became the UEFA Cup. Embarking on their first venture into this competition in 1983-84, Forest beat Vorwaerts and PSV Eindhoven before drawing Celtic. After a goalless draw at the City Ground, Forest turned in a marvellous performance at Parkhead to win 2-1. After beating Sturm Graz, Forest met Anderlecht in the semi-finals. In the first leg, two goals from Steve Hodge seemed to have put Forest through to the Final and a match with Spurs but the Belgians fought back to win 3-0 on their own soil.

Forest's next UEFA Cup campaign also floundered in Belgium, this time in the first round with FC Bruges winning 1-0 on aggregate.

In 1995-96, Forest beat Malmo, Auxerre and Lyon before losing to

Bayern Munich in the quarter-final, with the Germans winning the second leg at the City Ground 5-1.

UNDEFEATED

Nottingham Forest have remained undefeated at home throughout two Football League seasons, 1977-78 and 1978-79, although in seasons 1926-27 and 1953-54, the club were only defeated in their last home game of the campaign.

The club's best and longest undefeated home sequence in the Football League is of 51 matches from 27 April 1977 to 17 November 1979.

Forest's longest run of undefeated Football League matches, home and away is 42 between 26 November 1977 and 25 November 1978.

On 30 September 1978, their 2-1 win at Aston Villa had equalled Leeds United's record of 34 consecutive matches without defeat established in the 1968-69 and 1969-70 seasons.

UNUSUAL GOALS

Every Forest fan will have their own opinion as to which is the most unusual goal they have seen in a game involving the Reds.

On 7 May 1938, Forest travelled to Barnsley who were level on points with the City Ground club near the foot of the Second Division. The home side needed to win to avoid relegation and in doing so, would send Forest down to the Third Division.

Forest took the lead after 26 minutes through Martin but ten minutes before the break, Barnsley equalised when a spectacular shot from Asquith from almost 35 yards out bounced up on the bumpy pitch and shot over Ashton's left shoulder. Barnsley took the lead on the hour when Barlow's drive appeared to be almost thrown into his own net by Ashton!

Just when it looked as if Forest were down, came the most unusual goal of the match. Five minutes remained when a Reg Trim shot was saved by Binns in the Barnsley goal, who was then charged into by Martin. Binns was so shaken that both he and the ball were carried over the line. Th referee consulted his linesman and still gave a goal despite Barnsley's protests. When the final whistle went, Barnsley were down and Forest stayed up by the slimmest possible margin, one-200th part of a goal!

UTILITY PLAYERS

A utility player is one of those particularly gifted footballers who can play in several, or even many different positions.

One of Nottingham Forest's earliest utility players was Jack Armstrong. Extremely versatile, the Keyworth-born Armstrong appeared in every position for Forest except goalkeeper and full-back during his 18 years at the City Ground. Another Forest player to display his great versatility was Noah Burton who played in a variety of positions and was instrumental in the club winning the Second Division title in 1921-22.

After the mid-1960s, players were encouraged to become more adaptable and to see their role as less stereotyped. At the same time however, much less attention came to be paid to the implication of wearing a certain numbered shirt and accordingly, some of the more versatile players came to wear almost all the different numbered shirts at some stage or another, although this did not necessarily indicate a vast variety of positions.

Paul Richardson's lack of first team opportunities meant that the Shirebrook-born player had to be content with playing in a number of unfamiliar positions. In recent seasons, Lee Glover wore six different numbered shirts in Forest's cause.

V

VAN HOOIJDONK, PIERRE

Dutch World Cup star Pierre Van Hooijdonk began his career with NAC Breda before joining Celtic for a fee of £1.2 million in January 1995. At Parkhead he proved to be a prolific striker and had scored 58 goals in 89 games before falling out with the club and requesting a move. It looked as if he would join West Ham United but in March 1997 he signed for Nottingham Forest for a club record fee of £4.5 million.

After making his Premier League debut for the club in a 1-1 draw at Blackburn Rovers, it took him until his sixth game before he netted for Forest, despite linking well with Dean Saunders.

In 1997-98, Van Hooijdonk struck a fearsome partnership with

Kevin Campbell which netted 57 goals and secured an immediate return to the Premiership. Van Hooijdonk scored 34 of those goals including hat-tricks against Queen's Park Rangers (Home 4-0) and Charlton Athletic (Home 5-2). He was given a hero's chairlift around the pitch by Forest fans after the game against Reading which clinched the title in May.

Sadly in the summer of 1998, Van Hooijdonk delivered a devastating blow to Nottingham Forest's Premiership preparations by refusing to return to Britain while demanding a transfer. At the time of writing the club have agreed to let him leave the City Ground for a fee of £8 million.

VICTORIES

Nottingham Forest won 30 of their 46 Division Three (South) matches in 1950-51 and also achieved a record 70 points and a record total of 110 goals.

The club's highest victory in each of the major competitions is as follows:

Home

Football League	12-0 v Leicester Fosse	21 April 1909
FA Cup	7-2 v Sheffield Heeley	2 December 1882
Football League Cup	7-3 v Watford	10 November 1983

Away

Football League	7-1 v Port Vale	2 February 1957
	7-1 v Sheffield Wed	1 April 1995
FA Cup	14-0 v Clapton	17 January 1891
Football League Cup	7-0 v Bury	23 September 1980

Forest's poorest performance was in 1924-25 when they won only six matches out of their 42 League games and finished bottom of the First Division.

VICTORY SHIELD

As the First World war ended, Forest were Midland Section champions, one point clear of joint runners-up Birmingham and Notts County.

Everton, rated the best team of the time had won the Lancashire title, losing only one game, scoring 102 goals and collecting 52 points.

Marking the end of wartime football, the Victory Shield was contested by these two champions on a home and away basis. The first match at the City Ground on 10 May 1919 was witnessed by a crowd of 15,000 who saw the teams play out a goalless draw. The Shield seemed destined for the Merseyside club but seven days later the favourites were beaten in front of a 40,000 crowd at Goodison Park. The only goal of the game was scored by Noah Burton three minutes before half-time.

W

WALKER, BILLY

Billy Walker had a long and distinguished career in football, first as a player with Aston Villa (1919-33) and then as manager of Sheffield Wednesday (1933-37) and Chelmsford City (1938) before becoming boss of Nottingham Forest (1939-60).

Born in Wednesbury, Staffordshire on 29 October 1897, the son of a former Wolves full-back George Walker, he first played for Hednesford Town and Darlaston and was playing for Wednesbury Old Athletic when Aston Villa signed him on amateur forms in 1915.

A free-scoring inside-forward, he turned professional in 1919, making his Villa debut in the FA Cup tie against Queen's Park Rangers in 1920, a match in which he scored both goals in a 2-1 victory. He scored three more goals that season as Villa reached the FA Cup Final at Stamford Bridge, beating Huddersfield Town 1-0. The following season he scored 27 League goals and won his first England cap against Ireland at Sunderland. All told, he won 18 full caps. One of the finest players to pull on a Villa shirt, he played in 531 League and Cup games and scored 244 goals and was the first player to score a hat-trick of penalties in a League game.

He retired from the playing side of the game in December 1933, taking over as manager of Sheffield Wednesday, who were languishing near the foot of the table. By the end of the season he had guided them to mid-table safety. The following season he led them to third position in the First Division as well as winning the FA Cup but then things started to go wrong for him and after facing an angry group of shareholders, he resigned.

After a break from football he took over as manager of non-League

Chelmsford City but in March 1939 he began his long association with Nottingham Forest where he remained as manager until ill-health forced him to resign in 1960.

During his reign at the City Ground, Walker saw Forest relegated to the Third Division at the end of 1949, promoted as champions in 1950-51 and return to the First Division in 1957 for the first time in 32 years. He capped his career with victory in the 1959 FA Cup Final when Forest's 10 men held on to beat Luton Town 2-1.

Billy Walker's career had been an illustrious one and he remained a member of the Forest committee until his death at the age of 67 in 1964. Respected as a manager for his knowledge of the game and as a man for his integrity and honesty, Walker was one of the great figures of English football in the twentieth century who set the highest standards for himself and his teams.

WALKER, DES

Rejected by Tottenham Hotspur, Aston Villa and Birmingham City, Des Walker signed professional forms for Nottingham Forest in December 1983. He made his Leagued debut for the Reds in a 1-0 home win over Everton on 13 March 1984 and was immediately selected for the England Under-21 side.

Replacing Ian Butterworth in November 1985, the Hackney-born defender became a permanent fixture in the Forest side. Exceedingly fast, he began to display a maturity beyond his years and a coolness even in the most desperate of situations.

One of the best players ever to appear for the club, he made the first of his 47 international appearances whilst a Forest player against Denmark in 1989, coming on as a substitute for Arsenal's Tony Adams.

After appearing in 264 League games for Forest with just one goal, scored in the 1-1 home draw against Luton Town on New Years Day 1992, he signed for Italian club Sampdoria in May of that year. After only 30 League games for the Italian side he returned to England to sign for Sheffield Wednesday.

Capped 59 times by England, Walker has now played in 190 League games for the Owls.

The Unofficial A to Z

145

WALKER, HARRY

Goalkeeper Harry Walker was signed from Portsmouth in April 1947, having won an FA Cup winners' medal with the Fratton Park club in 1939. Making his Forest debut at Fulham on 26 May 1947, it soon became clear that the club had signed an excellent 'keeper.

He earned the nickname 'Mr Consistency' but even he could not stop the club's relegation at the end of the 1948-49 season.

He was an ever-present in 1950-51 when his goalkeeping had as much to do with Forest winning the Division Three (South) championship as it did with Wally Ardron's 36 goals.

He remained first-close 'keeper at the City Ground until 1955, playing his last match in a 4-1 defeat at Notts County on 12 February. Injury eventually forced his retirement from the game.

WALLACE, BOB

Though he was born in Greenock, Bob Wallace played his early football in Ireland with Linfield. He spent two and a half years with the Irish club, eventually captaining them before joining Nottingham Forest in the summer of 1923.

Making his debut in the opening game of the following season, a 2-1 defeat at Everton, he went on to appear in 107 consecutive League matches - the only Forest player to make over one hundred consecutive appearances from debut.

A natural left-half, he formed a good half-back line with another former Linfield player and Irish international Gerry Morgan and Jack Belton. As at Linfield he was eventually appointed as Forest's captain and continued playing at left-half until 1931, when he played the last of his 269 League and Cup games at Stoke on 17 January.

WARTIME FOOTBALL

First World War: In spite of the outbreak of war in 1914, the major football leagues embarked upon their planned programme of matches for the ensuing season and these were completed at the end of April the following year. The season saw the club finish 18th in the Second Division, losing their last match 7-0 at Arsenal.

Many players lost some of their best years of their careers and Forest lost some of their best years as well. In 1915-16, Forest finished first in both the Principal and Subsidiary Tournaments of the Midlands Section, with the 8-1 win over Chesterfield in which William Birch scored four goals, being their highest victory. Forest won the Principal Tournament of the Midland

Section in 1918-19 the last season of wartime regional football before returning to League action the following season when they again finished 18th in the Second Division!

Second World War: In contrast to the events of 1914, once war was declared on 3 September 1939, the Football League programme of 1939-40 was immediately suspended and the government forbade any major sporting events, so that for a while there was no football of any description. Forest had opened the season with a 4-1 reversal at Barnsley, following it with two home wins over Newcastle United 2-0 and Newport County 2-1. Like most other clubs, they then arranged local friendly matches.

On 21 October 1939, Forest in common with other League clubs began regional competitive football.

There were some very interesting results. In 1940-41, Forest beat Walsall 8-4 at the City Ground and then 7-6 at Fellowes Park with Broome scoring four of the goals. Lincoln City too provided good opposition. Forest went down 6-5 at Sincil Bank with Collins netting four of the goals but gained revenge two seasons later with an 8-1 home win, with both Beaumont and Flewitt grabbing hat-tricks.

WEATHER CONDITIONS

When Forest played Southampton in the FA Cup semi-final replay in March 1898, the Southern League champions were beaten 2-0 thanks to two last-minute goals by McInnes and Richards. At the end of the game Southampton protested fiercely, because the replay had been held up by a snowstorm and in their opinion the game should never have been restarted. But it was all to no avail and Forest went on to win the FA Cup for the first time in their history, beating Derby County 3-1.

In complete contrast, when Forest visited Grimsby Town on 1 September 1906 for the first game of the season, they went down 3-1 on what is thought to be the hottest day a League programme has ever been completed – the temperature was over 90F (32C).

WEBB, NEIL

The son of a former Reading forward Doug Webb, he followed his father to Elm Park, signing professional forms in 1980. In July 1982 he joined Portsmouth, where he began to produce some outstanding displays in midfield. After playing in 123 League games for the Fratton Park club he signed for Forest in June 1985 and made his debut against Luton Town on the opening day of the 1985-86 season.

An important member of Forest's midfield, he was also a regular goalscorer and netted hat-tricks against Coventry City (Home 5-2 on 1 January 1986) and Chelsea (Away 6-2 on 20 September 1986).

He made his England debut against West Germany in 1988 and won 18 caps during his four seasons at the City Ground. When his contract expired in 1989, a tribunal set a fee of £1.5 million, which

Neil Webb

Manchester United were more than happy to meet. Hampered by injuries in his first seasons at Old Trafford, he came back to gain an FA Cup winners' medal in 1990 and make an appearance in that year's World Cup finals.

He returned to the City Ground for a second spell in October 1992 and played in a further 30 League games over the next two seasons. After a loan spell at Swindon Town he joined Grimsby Town before playing non-League football with Aldershot.

WEST, ENOCH

Enoch 'Knocker' West played his early football with Sheffield United but in 1905, a ridiculously low fee of just £5 was enoughto persuade the Bramall Lane club to part with their man to Nottingham Forest.

He made his debut in the fourth game of the 1905-06 season, a 3-2 win over Bury at the City Ground. Linking well with Grenville Morris he appeared in every forward position for the Reds and in 1907-08 was the First Division's leading scorer with 26 goals including all four in the 4-1 home win over Sunderland and hat-tricks against Chelsea (Home 6-0) and Blackburn Rovers (Away 3-3) He was the club's leading scorer again the following season but at the end of the 1909-10 season after he had scored 100 goals in 183 League and Cup games he joined Manchester United.

He scored on his debut in a 2-1 win at Woolwich Arsenal, the first of many goals that helped United to their second League title in four seasons. In April 1915 he was found guilty of helping to 'fix' a game against Liverpool and was suspended for life along with other players. His ban, the longest in Football League history was eventually lifted in November 1945, after 30 years.

WHARE, BILL

Guernsey-born Bill Whare was recommended to Nottingham Forest by a former colleague of manager Billy Walker. He signed professional forms for the Reds in May 1947 and made his League debut at left-half in a 2-2 draw at home to Spurs two years later,

However it was at right-back that he was to become a permanent fixture in the Forest side. Indeed his performances in the number two shirt were so outstanding that the only way the previous occupant Geoff Thomas could get back in the side was at left-back.

He only scored two goals in his Forest career - the winner against Huddersfield Town on 4 October 1952 and the final goal in Forest's 4-1 win over Aston Villa on 23 November 1958.

Serving the club throughout the 1950s, he won a Third Division (South) championship medal in 1950-51 and helped the club to promotion in 1956- 7 before appearing in Forest's FA Cup Final success of 1959.

WHITEFOOT, JEFF

One of the original 'Busby Babes' Jeff Whitefoot was the youngest player to make a League appearance for Manchester United at 16 years 105 days when he played against Portsmouth in April 1950.

After winning a League Championship medal in 1955-56 he lost his place to Eddie Colman and in 1957 he moved to Grimsby Town. At Old Trafford he had won an England Under-23 cap against Italy and it was clear that the Blundell Park club would have difficulty holding on to this powerful wing-half.

So it proved for in the summer of 1958 he signed for Nottingham Forest. Replacing Bill Morley, he made his debut in a disastrous 5-1 defeat at Wolves on the opening day of the 1958-59 season but ended the campaign with an FA Cup winners' medal. During his ten seasons with the club he had two fairly lengthy spells out of the first team but still appeared in 285 League and Cup games before losing his place to Henry Newton during the 1966-67 season. Injury forced the Cheadle-born player to retire in 1968.

WIDDOWSON, SAM

Born at Hucknall Torkard in April 1851, Sam Widdowson was the man most responsible for the survival and progress of Nottingham Forest in the club's early years.

A great innovator, he was given the credit for the creation of the formation of two full-backs, three half-backs and five forwards, for until then clubs played in a 2-2-6 formation. In 1874 he caused great amazement when he played for Forest in modified cricket pads to protect his shins from the opponents' tactic of 'hacking'.

He first played for Forest in 1869 and remained a permanent fixture in the side for 16 years until his retirement in 1885. A supreme footballer, Widdowson's services were always in demand by other local clubs and occasionally he turned out for Notts in games of importance. From 1879 to 1884 he served as the club's chairman before later becoming a member of the FA Council and helping to select the England team.

Typical of the man, in 1888 he left his sick bed to attend an international trial game and finding that one side was a player short, he borrowed a pair of boots and played an outstanding game at full-back!

WIGHTMAN, HARRY

The first man to hold the title of team manager at Nottingham Forest, he signed for Chesterfield when he was 17 and during the First World War spent four seasons at the City Ground. However in May 1919 he joined Derby County and went on to make 189 appearances for the Rams at centre-half and full-back before becoming assistant to Derby manager George Jobey.

In May 1929 he rejoined his first club Chesterfield before spells at Notts County and Luton Town. At Kenilworth Road he laid the foundations for future success, for in 1936-37, the Hatters won the Third Division (South) title. By then though, Wightman had left after he had a difference of opinion with his directors. Wightman was briefly with Mansfield Town but soon left to take up the manager's post at the City Ground.

Wightman's three seasons in charge at Forest were not successful ones as the club went close to relegation on each occasion, finishing 18th, 20th and 20th again. It came as no surprise that in March 1939, Harry Wightman and Nottingham Forest parted company.

WIGNALL, FRANK

Playing his early football with Horwich RMI in the Lancashire Combination, the Blackrod-born forward joined Everton in May 1958 and made 33 League appearances for the Toffees before signing for Forest in April 1963 for a then club record fee of £20,000.

Making his debut for the Reds in the opening game of the 1963-64 season, he ended the campaign as the club's top scorer with 16 goals including a hat-trick in the 3-2 win at Bolton Wanderers, the club he had supported as a boy.

He was capped twice by England in 1964, scoring both goals on his debut as England beat Wales 2-1. Later that year he broke his leg in a County cup-tie and only managed to play in 19 games during the following season. In 1966-67 he was back to his best, acting as the perfect foil to Joe Baker. The goals seemed to dry up in 1967-68 and in March of that season he was allowed to join Wolves. After just 32 League appearances for the Molineux club he joined Derby County and helped the Rams to win the Second Division championship. He ended his League career with Mansfield Town before playing non-

League football for King's Lynn and Burton Albion. He later coached the Qatar national side and managed Shepshed Charterhouse.

WILSON, TOMMY

A centre-forward with Forest from 1951 to 1960, Tommy Wilson made 217 League and Cup appearances for them, scoring 89 goals before finishing his career with Walsall.

Born in Bedlington in September 1930, Wilson signed for Forest from Cinderhill Colliery in April 1951. Originally an outside-right, he made his debut in the number seven shirt in October 1951 in a 2-0 home win over Luton Town. During his first three seasons however, he was kept out of the side by Alan Moore but in the final two games of 1953-54, manager Billy Walker tried him at inside-forward and from then until his move to Walsall, he was a Forest regular.

Wilson made his mark in 1956-57 when he scored 14 goals in 32 appearances during Forest's successful promotion campaign. Although on the small side for a centre-forward, just 5ft 8ins and weighing under 12 stone, his speed and control made him a handful for First Division defences and over the next three seasons, he topped the club's scoring lists.

The pinnacle of Tommy Wilson's career came in May 1959 when a 10-man Forest side held on to beat Luton 2-1 in a thrilling FA Cup Final. He had scored some vital goals on the way to Wembley, none more so than the strike which earned a replay against Birmingham City in round five and the two which defeated cup holders Bolton Wanderers in round six. In the final, Wilson got his head to a Billy Gray cross to put the Reds two up after only 14 minutes.

In September 1960, Wilson played his last game for the Reds in a 2-0 home defeat by Newcastle United. He moved on to Walsall in 1960, helping them to promotion from Division Three in his first season and ending his League career there in 1962.

WINFIELD, JOHN

Signing as a full-time professional in May 1960, a year after he had joined the club, he made his League debut for the Reds in a 4-3 home defeat by Blackpool on 3 February 1962. Initially his appearances at the City Ground were restricted by Henry Newton and Calvin Palmer and it was only after moving to left-back that he became a first team regular.

A tough-tackling defender with a good distribution, he played in 410 League and Cup games before leaving Forest at the end of the 1973-74 season. He had become a target for a certain section of the Forest fans and jumped at the opportunity of joining his former colleague John Barnwell at Peterborough United.

WITHE, PETER

Liverpool-born Peter Withe played his early football with Smith Coggins FC before signing for Southport in August 1971. After four months at Haig Avenue he joined Barrow but in 1972 he was released.

He then played for Portland Timbers in the United States and Port Elizabeth and Arcadia Shepherds in South Africa before returning to these shores in November 1973. He made a few appearances for Wolverhampton Wanderers before joining Birmingham City in 1975. A year later he signed for Nottingham Forest. A big, strong target-man, he made his debut for the Reds in a 5-1 win over Carlisle United on 25 September 1976, scoring the last goal.

Linking well with Tony Woodcock, he headed the club's goalscoring charts in 1976-77 with 16 League goals as the club won promotion from the Second Division. This successful pairing continued to terrorise defences and in 1977-78, he scored 12 League goals including all four in a 4-0 win over Ipswich Town, as Forest won the League Championship.

After scoring 39 goals in 99 League and Cup games, this 'happy wanderer' left the City Ground to join Newcastle United. In May 1980 he joined Aston Villa where he had the best years of his career, scoring the winner in the 1982 European Cup Final win over Hamburg and winning 11 England caps.

He later played for Sheffield United, Birmingham City (again) and Huddersfield Town where he was appointed as the Terriers assistant-manager. Appointed first team coach, he later managed Wimbledon before returning to Villa Park as the club's chief scout.

Peter Withe, who formed a prolific goalscoring partnership with Tony Woodcock.

WOAN, IAN

Starting as an associated schoolboy with Everton, he later went into non-League football with Heswall, Caernarfon, Newton and Runcorn, from where Nottingham Forest signed him in March 1990.

He made his Forest debut as a substitute in a 6-2 victory at Norwich City on 2 January 1991. By the end of that season, he had won a regular place in the Reds' line-up on the left-wing and scored three gaols, including a superb volley against Liverpool to end their Championship hopes.

A surprise selection for the 1991 FA Cup Final, it wasn't until 1994-95 that the Wirrall-born winger established himself as a regular in the Forest side. Despite struggling to make much of an impression over the last two seasons, he has scored 31 goals in 208 League outings for the City Ground club.

WOODCOCK, TONY

After making his Forest debut on 24 April 1974 in a 3-1 defeat at Aston Villa, he was given little opportunity in the first team and in 1976 had loan spells at Lincoln City and Doncaster Rovers.

In November of that year, Brian Clough called him into the first team for the Anglo-Scottish Cup match against Ayr United. He scored one of the goals in Forest's 2-0 second-leg win and went on to become an important member of the Reds' promotion squad, scoring 11 goals in 30 League games.

He proved the perfect foil to Peter Withe and in 1977-78 when Forest won the League Championship, both strikers scored 19 League and Cup goals. Following Withe's departure, Woodcock continued to link well with Birtles and continued scoring goals including a hattrick in a 3-1 win over Middlesborough at Ayresome Park on 25 September 1979.

In November 1980 after winning six England caps, he joined German club FC Cologne. Two years later he returned to England to play with Arsenal. He made 131 League appearances for the Gunners, scoring 56 goals before returning to play for Cologne in 1986.

Tony Woodcock, on his way to scoring one of his 36 league goals for Fǿrest.

Ian Wallace, who came close to scoring for Forest during the World Club Championship.

WORLD CLUB CHAMPIONSHIPS

On 11 February 1981, Forest played Nacional of Uruguay in Tokyo for the World Club Championship. Nacional took the lead after only 10 minutes when Moreira out-paced Frank Gray before crossing to Victorino to shoot past Peter Shilton. The Uruguayans had the ball in the net a second time from the boot of Bica but Victorino had strayed offside and the goal disallowed. In the second-half, Forest did a lot of attacking, with Ian Wallace hitting the side netting and John Robertson heading wide from a good position. As the Uruguayans sat back, soaking up a lot of Forest pressure, Stuart Gray headed a Robertson cross against the post and Forest's Scottish international winger had a shot cleared off the line in the final seconds.

WORLD WIDE WEB

The unofficial web site for Nottingham Forest is at:

http://www.ccc.nottingham.ac.uk/~ccznffc/NFFC.html

Just like this book, it has no official connection with the club!

WORST STARTS

The club's worst ever start to a season was in 1929-30. It took 11 League games to record the first victory of the season, drawing four and losing six of the opening ten fixtures. The run ended with a 1-0 win at Reading on 19 October 1929 with Johnny Dent the scorer.

X

XMAS DAY

There was a time when football matches were regularly played on Christmas Day but in recent years, the game's authorities have dropped the fixture from their calendar.

The last time Nottingham Forest played on Christmas Day was in 1957 when they beat Newcastle United 4-1 at St James' Park with Imlach 2, Wilson and Baily scoring for the Reds.

There have been some memorable Christmas Day games, perhaps

none more so than 1943 when an understrength Forest side lost 9-1 at Northampton Town!

On Christmas Day 1953, a Wally Ardron hat-trick helped Forest defeat Leeds United 5-2, whilst another Christmas Day hat-trick was scored by Jack Spaven when Forest beat Rotherham United 6-1 in 1920.

Forest's main opponents over the years on Christmas Day have been Notts County. The two sides first met on a Christmas Day in 1903 when County won 1-0 at the City Ground. The Meadow Lane side also won their sixth and last Christmas Day meeting in 1940, winning 4-2 in front of a City Ground crowd of 2,266. Forest did have two successes in between, winning 1-0 in 1917 and 2-0 in 1918.

YOUNGEST

The youngest player to appear for Nottingham Forest is Stephen Burke who was 16 years 22 days old when he played in the 2-1 home win over Ayr United in the first-leg of the semi-final of the Anglo-Scottish Cup on 20 October 1976.

ZENITH

Few fans will argue over which moment has been the finest in the club's history. The appointment of Brian Clough as manager paved the way for the formation of a Forest side that won the League Championship in 1978 and the European Cup in the next two years.

ZENITH DATA SYSTEMS CUP

The Zenith Data Systems Cup replaced the Simod Cup for the 1989-90 season. Forest's first match in the competition saw them beat Manchester City 3-2 at the City Ground with goals from Pearce (pen) Carr and Crosby but then despite Pearce scoring again in the next round, they went out 2-1 at Aston Villa.

The Reds went out at a similar stage in 1990-91, for after beating Newcastle United 2-1, they lost by a similar scoreline at Barnsley with Steve Chettle netting for Forest.

In 1991-92 Forest won their second round tie at Elland Road, beating Leeds United 3-1 with Teddy Sheringham scoring two of the goals, one of them a penalty. Drawn away to Aston Villain the quarter-finals, goals from Pearce and Woan gave Forest a comfortable passage to the last four in the Northern Section. Facing Tranmere Rovers at Prenton Park, a Roy Keane double gave Forest a 2-0 win and a two-legged Northern Section Final against Leicester City.

A Scot Gemmill goal gave Forest a 1-1 draw at Filbert Street before goals from Crosby and Wassall gave them a 2-0 win and a place in the final at Wembley.

In an exciting match in front of a 67,688 Wembley crowd, Forest beat Southampton 3-2 with two goals from Scot Gemmill and one from Kingsley Black.

We publish a wide range of sports, leisure and local interest books covering most of Britain. Here is a small selection:

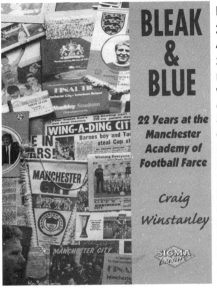

BLEAK & BLUE:
22 YEARS AT THE MANCHESTER ACADEMY OF FOOTBALL FARCE
30,000 people can't be wrong - or maybe they can! Craig Winstanley writes his heartfelt account of what could again be a great football club! **Share the joys and misery** of two decades spent in supporting Manchester City Football Club. **Boggle at the Blues record**: fifteen managers, two cup finals, two promotions and three relegations. **A big book in every way!** All major games covered in relentless detail. **Hugely entertaining:** you'll laugh, you'll cry - mostly the latter! *£8.95!*

COME ON CYMRU!
FOOTBALL IN WALES
"Keith Haynes is the Welsh Nick Hornby . . . you won't put this book down until you've read it from cover to cover." - *Future* magazine. **The first book** to be written by fans of Welsh football for football fans everywhere. **Includes contributions** from leading Welsh fanzine writers. **The highs and the lows** of Welsh football, nationally and internationally. **An entertaining read** - even for non-Welsh-football supporters! £6.95

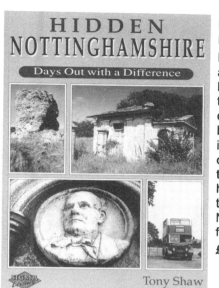

HIDDEN NOTTINGHAMSHIRE: DAYS OUT WITH A DIFFERENCE

Local historian and amateur archaeologist Tony Shaw has turned his attention to Nottinghamshire in this fascinating new book. Both county residents and tourists will now be able to discover 100 places of interest which do not feature in any other guidebook: a tiny Robin Hood theatre, a holy well, King John's hunting lodge and hexagonal toll-house. You'll be amazed at what Nottinghamshire has been hiding from you for so long!

£6.95

COVER UNDER CONSTRUCTION

BEST TEA SHOP WALKS IN NOTTINGHAMSHIRE

This new guide by Paul and Sandra Biggs features 25 enticing walks, and is the perfect way to discover Nottinghamshire's finest countryside.

Packed with fascinating facts about the county including the history of the Bramley Apple and Southwell Minster, this book has it all - and more! With walks ranging from 2-9 miles, detailed walking instructions, clear maps and attractive photographs, each route contains details of a charming tea shop stop.

£6.95 (Due Summer 1999)

PUB WALKS *in* NOTTINGHAMSHIRE

ABIGAIL BRISTOW • NORMAN JAMES
CHRIS ROBSON • MARTIN SMITH

PUB WALKS IN NOTTINGHAMSHIRE

Hill walks, riverside rambles or village strolls: Nottinghamshire has so much to offer the discerning walker.

This well-established guidebook covers the entire county, discovering excellent walks and authentic country pubs that welcome ramblers. Written by an enthusiastic team of walkers and real-ale experts - Les Lumsdon, Abigail Bristow, Chris Robson and Martin Smith - you'll soon discover the real Nottinghamshire countryside.

£6.95

OLD NOTTINGHAMSHIRE *remembered*

KEITH TAYLOR

OLD NOTTINGHAMSHIRE REMEMBERED

Local historian Keith Taylor has compiled this fascinating set of recollections.

Read about how people lived over a hundred years ago: a peep into the stately homes and more humble residences of the county, illustrated with period photographs.

"Essential reading"
HERITAGE NEWSPAPERS (Birmingham).

£7.95

INTERNATIONAL LINE DANCE FAVORITES

The follow-up to the sell-out "UK Line Dance Favourites" this new dance package is crammed full with clear, tried and tested instructions for all the current UK favourites PLUS an international selection. Carefully graded from dance to dance, "International Line Dance Favorites" features the authors' own unique system of step-by-step instructions, taking line dancing into the year 2000! Suitable for all - from beginners to experienced dancers - the book also features a FREE CD from the world's leading country music dance artist - **Scooter Lee.**

£10.95 *(including FREE CD)*